Ars Celebrandi

Celebrating and Concelebrating Mass

Father Paul Turner

Foreword by Bishop Mark Seitz

LITURGICAL PRESS
Collegeville, Minnesota

www.litpress.org

Nihil Obstat: Rev. Robert Harren, J.C.L., *Censor Deputatus.*

Imprimatur: ✠ Most Rev. Donald J. Kettler, J.C.L., D.D.,
Bishop of St. Cloud, March 25, 2021.

Cover design by Monica Bokinskie. Cover photo courtesy of Getty Images.
Interior art by Frank Kacmarcik, OblSB.

2 3 4 5 6 7 8 9

Library of Congress Cataloging-in-Publication Data

Names: Turner, Paul, 1953– author.
Title: Ars celebrandi : celebrating and concelebrating mass / Paul Turner.
Description: Collegeville, Minnesota : Liturgical Press, [2021] | Summary: "Reviews standard principles to guide priests in celebrating the Mass and offers suggestions for how to improve their presiding at Mass. This comprehensive resource looks beyond rubrics to styles of presiding and reflects on certain principles that will help to foster participation while leading prayer"— Provided by publisher.
Identifiers: LCCN 2020045122 (print) | LCCN 2020045123 (ebook) | ISBN 9780814666432 (paperback) | ISBN 9780814666456 (epub) | ISBN 9780814666456 (mobi) | ISBN 9780814666456 (pdf)
Subjects: LCSH: Mass—Celebration. | Concelebration.
Classification: LCC BX2230.3 .T856 2021 (print) | LCC BX2230.3 (ebook) | DDC 264/.36—dc23
LC record available at https://lccn.loc.gov/2020045122
LC ebook record available at https://lccn.loc.gov/2020045123

"Fr. Paul Turner explores the rubrics of the Mass and its unwritten elements to assist presiders to access, and lead the faithful into, the full richness of the liturgy they celebrate. Written with charity and clarity, *Ars Celebrandi* will give all who care about the Mass a deepened understanding of the 'noble simplicity of the Roman rite.'"

— Letitia Thornton, Director, Office of Worship, Diocese of Boise

"In one inspiring volume, Father Turner reviews countless details which impact the art of celebration. Instead of engaging in liturgical debates, the author consistently shows a deep respect for the Order of Mass, the General Instruction of the Roman Missal, and the beauty of the liturgical texts. He combines sound theology and liturgical history with logic, reason, humor, and a generous helping of pastoral advice. This book should become mandatory reading in every seminary and a thoughtful 'examen' every time one prepares to lead God's people in the church's liturgy."

— Rita A. Thiron
Executive Director, Federation of Diocesan Liturgical Commissions

"In addressing this important task of liturgical presiding, Father Paul Turner offers more than just a 'how to do it' guide through the liturgy. Rather, he points to a foundational vision for the *Ars Celebrandi*—a way of thinking about it—with keen insight into the inner disposition necessary to celebrate the liturgy authentically and well. This foundational understanding, then, is woven into a well-grounded hermeneutic of the rites as they are now given to us and undergirds the practical, concrete, and detailed recommendations that follow. This has long been needed and will be an important addition to the library of every liturgical minister."

— Rev. R. Bruce Cinquegrani, D. Min.
Pastor, St. Anne Catholic Church, Memphis, Tennessee

"As a seminary professor who teaches candidates for the priesthood how to celebrate Mass, Father Paul Turner's comprehensive guide is the course textbook I've been searching for, for years! He expertly presents the many theological, spiritual, pastoral, and rubrical considerations which, together, make up the priestly *ars celebrandi*. Throughout, the importance of celebrating the sacred mysteries with faithfulness, artistic sensitivity, and pastoral care is made with clarity and precision. Seminarians and seasoned presiders alike will benefit greatly from this thoughtful, detailed, and approachable study of the priestly *ars celebrandi*."

— Father Matthew Ernest, STD, Director and Professor of Liturgy, Saint Joseph's Seminary (Dunwoodie); Director of the Office of Liturgy, Archdiocese of New York

HOC VOLVMEN DEDICAT AVCTOR

THOMÆ TVRNER MARIÆQVE SIMENTAL

QVI MISSAM CATHOLICAM ATQVE MVNVS CHRISTIANVM AMANT

QVI PLENE CONSCIE ET ACTVOSE IN EISDEM PARTICIPVNT

QVI SACERDOTES QVALIS ILLVM FOVENT

ATQVE IVSTE CVPIENT

VT ISTI MELIVS FACIANT

Contents

Foreword

What a pleasure and honor it is to be writing a foreword for a book by the Rev. Paul Turner. For a number of years, he has been my guru and go-to source in matters liturgical. He brings true scholarship and an impressive body of knowledge together with down-to-earth pastoral experience in his daily service as a parish priest. No pie-in-the-sky theoretician, he.

Most people know me today as bishop of a border diocese, the Diocese of El Paso, and for various efforts in which I have participated in the area of social justice. However, in a former life I studied liturgy and taught for a number of years while I was on the formation team at Holy Trinity Seminary at the University of Dallas. That work came before my nineteen years of service as a parish pastor. My love of the church's worship and my concern for the fruitful celebration of the liturgy never left me.

As a bishop I have come to believe with even greater conviction that one of the most fruitful undertakings that could be promoted for the renewal of the church would be to simply learn to celebrate the liturgy better. Nearly sixty years after the much-needed reform of the liturgy, we find ourselves with new rites, new texts, but sadly unreformed understandings and priorities.

What a treasure we have in the liturgy, this life-giving gift bestowed upon the church by Christ himself! I have often observed with all sincerity that everything I ever learned about the practice of the faith and particularly about social justice I learned at the altar of God, in the celebration of the liturgy. As we have often heard, "the liturgy is the summit toward which the activity of the church is directed; it is also the source from which all its power flows" (*Sacrosanctum Concilium*, 10). These are far more than mere high-sounding words. All that the church is and does is summed up in the action we call worship. In our act of worship within the church we become our truest self; we are transformed and nourished that we might do the work of Christ and make him present in the world.

The liturgy of the church is thus an inestimable treasure, the very heart of our life as sons and daughters of God. It is in the liturgy that we discover the seed of Catholic teaching and the grace to live as Christ taught us. All the actions of the church and of the Christian have their source and their highest expression there. As the ancient dictum says, *Lex orandi, lex credendi*. To translate this phrase loosely, but I think accurately, "The church's worship is the source of the church's belief." Taking this a step further, we can say that all social action undertaken by the Catholic Christian is done under the impulse of what we have received in worship and also leads us back to worship.

Accepting this, no further arguments are needed to make clear why we must all do our utmost to worship faithfully and well. The liturgy deserves the attention of the members of the church and their best efforts. If that is the case for all the members, then how much more is this true of those ordained to the ministerial priesthood. Those of us who are ordained to the priesthood find our deepest identity in the act of worship. We are ordained to lead the members of the church in the praise of God and every other aspect of our service grows out of this one reason for our being.

These days we rightly eschew any implication that the liturgy is the private purview of the priest. No! The liturgy is the action of the entire people of God who are being more perfectly formed into the Body of Christ. The Second Vatican Council's seminal teaching that the people of God are called to full, conscious, and active participation is based upon this fundamental recognition. At the same time, we cannot deny that at the liturgy there is no one who has a more profound impact upon the celebration than the priest whose task it is to bring "holy order" to the gathered assembly. The document of the US bishops says this succinctly and well: "No other single factor affects the Liturgy as much as the attitude, style, and bearing of the priest celebrant, who 'prays in the name of the Church and of the assembled community' " (*Sing to the Lord, 18–19*).

The liturgy, as we know, is a language and a certain style of communication that comes down to us from the ages but is also constantly adapting under the guidance of the Spirit in every age. It is a language of signs and symbols that are read universally by people in the church. To be sure, there are regional and cultural aspects that are rightly represented as local communities worship, but these are secondary to the expressions that unite us across times and places. It is of great importance that we ourselves understand the "language" of the symbols.

It serves us well to give attention to the "grammar" of this language from time to time. The church is not looking for rigid robotic uniformity. Each community will very rightly incarnate the liturgy according to their own place and time, but hopefully not in a way that seems to make the liturgy more about them than about God.

This is particularly the case in regard to each priest's style, his *ars celebrandi*. The way a priest celebrates should allow him to be more and more transparent as an instrument of God. God wants to use the priest and to use his gifts to make him a sign of Christ present in the flesh presiding at our act of worship.

In our effort to "do what the church does" and to allow the Lord to be present, we should see the rubrics as helpful and necessary guides to the effective and faithful celebration of the liturgy. The rubrics are like the directions that come with recipes. Unless you are a very experienced cook, you would be foolish to try to bake without them. If I might continue the cooking analogy, we could say the rubrics allow us to cook up a dish that all can recognize as the irreplaceable food that Christ continues to prepare and to serve the people of the church.

And so, I would like to commend you to the guidance of the Master Liturgical Chef, Fr. Paul Turner. If you take the time to reflect upon your own *ars celebrandi* in light of his careful analysis as I have, you will find that you are personally challenged to rededicate yourself to the mysteries you celebrate and to employ the full richness of the renewed Roman Rite. The sacramental signs that you enact will reveal their power, and the transformative work of Jesus Christ will unfold in your life and the life of the community you serve.

Most Rev. Mark J. Seitz, DD
Bishop of the Diocese of El Paso

Acknowledgments

I wish to thank
The priests of the dioceses of Norwich, St. Augustine, Wollongong, Antigonish, and Sale, who listened,
The monks of Conception Abbey, who inspired,
The faculty of Kenrick Seminary, who taught,
Bishop Mark Seitz, Father Bruce Cinquegrani, and Tish Thornton, who read,
Fathers Michael Driscoll, Ken Riley and Michael Witczak, who advised,
The blog followers, who asked,
The people of the Cathedral of the Immaculate Conception, who waited,
God, who authors.

P.T.

Introduction

Irony

"I am suspending the celebration of public Masses throughout the diocese." The announcement on March 17, 2020, surely shocked the priests of the Diocese of Sale, Australia, but they barely flinched. Bishop Patrick O'Regan was departing shortly for Sydney to attend a meeting with other members of the Australian hierarchy to discuss among other topics how to respond to the COVID-19 pandemic. The unprecedented suspension of public celebrations of the Mass responded to directives from civic authorities to limit public gatherings in an extraordinary effort to stem the spread of the contagious and deadly virus.

The bishop's announcement came just before the lunch break at a workshop I was presenting to his priests that day. I had set aside three weeks for a series of lectures in six different Australian dioceses, including the National Biennial Liturgy Conference in Parramatta. After Brisbane and Sale, I'd intended to speak in Melbourne, Adelaide and Perth.

When the Sale priests regathered after lunch, I turned my attention to the announced topic: *ars celebrandi*. The irony hit me hard. The bishop had just told his priests that for the foreseeable future they could not preside at Mass in public, and my task was now to suggest how to improve their presiding at Mass in public. I acknowledged the situation, shared a moment of sorrow with them, and pressed on.

My hosts and I canceled the rest of my talks. I flew back to my diocese in the United States and put myself into a fourteen-day quarantine away from my residence, to make sure I was healthy enough to go back inside the building that serves as both home and office for several people, all of whom use the same kitchen.

With time on my hands, at the midpoint of Lent 2020, I turned to the book I'd promised Liturgical Press that I would begin after Easter. That would be this one. The same topic, *ars celebrandi*, seems out of place amid the other concerns facing the world.

Still, I pray that by the time this book sees the light of day, priests will have returned to presider's chairs and the faithful will have filled the nave. Perhaps after a hiatus, priests may consider afresh some principles for presiding at Mass. If so, I hope this book will help.

Ars Celebrandi

Literally, *ars celebrandi* means "the art of celebrating." It implies that presiding over the liturgy takes more than following instructions. It requires a certain style.

Pope Benedict XVI highlighted the expression in the year 2007 within his postsynodal exhortation *Sacramentum Caritatis*,[1] and the concept has drawn more attention in the intervening years. The pope was responding to the 2005 synod of bishops, which itself had gathered following the Vatican-promoted 2004 Year of the Eucharist.

Pope Benedict addressed *ars celebrandi* in the second part of his exhortation, "The Eucharist, a Mystery to Be Celebrated." He laid out the classical balance of prayer and belief, and he exhorted the role of beauty in the liturgy as an expression of God's mysterious glory. He reminded readers that the subject of the liturgy's intrinsic beauty is Christ himself, who includes his body the church in his work. The celebration of the Eucharist implies a living tradition from the time of St. Paul (1 Cor 11:23), Benedict continued, and the church cannot change its basic structure.[2]

These preliminary arguments set up Pope Benedict's paragraphs on *ars celebrandi*:

> In the course of the Synod, there was frequent insistence on the need to avoid any antithesis between the *ars celebrandi*, the art of

[1] Post-Synodal Apostolic Exhortation *Sacramentum Caritatis* of the Holy Father Benedict XVI to the Bishops, Clergy, Consecrated Persons and the Lay Faithful on the Eucharist as the Source and Summit of the Church's Life and Mission (February 22, 2007), http://www.vatican.va/content/benedict-xvi/en/apost_exhortations/documents/hf_ben-xvi_exh_20070222_sacramentum-caritatis.html.

[2] *Sacramentum Caritatis*, 34–37.

> proper celebration, and the full, active and fruitful participation of all the faithful. The primary way to foster the participation of the People of God in the sacred rite is the proper celebration of the rite itself. The *ars celebrandi* is the best way to ensure their *actuosa participatio*. The *ars celebrandi* is the fruit of faithful adherence to the liturgical norms in all their richness; indeed, for two thousand years this way of celebrating has sustained the faith life of all believers, called to take part in the celebration as the People of God, a royal priesthood, a holy nation (cf. 1 Pet 2:4-5, 9).[3]

When the pope translated *ars celebrandi* inside this paragraph, he used a dynamic equivalence, rather than a strict adherence to the Latin phrase. He called it not "the art of celebrating," but "the art of proper celebration." The insertion of the word "proper" stresses ritual fidelity, and the change from "celebrating" to "celebration" applies the term to aspects beyond the behavior of the priest. Nonetheless, Pope Benedict forged an important link between proper celebration and the active participation of the people: A good *ars celebrandi* is the fruit of adhering to liturgical norms. That, he argues, will in turn enhance participation.

Bishops, priests, and deacons have a specific responsibility, Pope Benedict wrote, especially the bishop who is to ensure unity and harmony in the liturgy of his territory. His celebrations at the cathedral are to be carried out "with complete respect for the *ars celebrandi*," and are thus models for the diocese.[4] His liturgies are to reflect not just any style of celebrating, but "the art of proper celebration."

Only then did Pope Benedict detail the implications. *Ars celebrandi* includes liturgical norms, a sense of the sacred, outward signs, the harmony of the rite, liturgical vestments, furnishings, sacred space, and propagation of the General Instruction of the Roman Missal (GIRM) and the Order of Readings for Mass. Equally important, he says,

> is an attentiveness to the various kinds of language that the liturgy employs: words and music, gestures and silence, movement, the liturgical colors of the vestments. By its very nature the liturgy operates on different levels of communication which

[3] *Sacramentum Caritatis*, 38.

[4] *Sacramentum Caritatis*, 39.

> enable it to engage the whole human person. The simplicity of its gestures and the sobriety of its orderly sequence of signs communicate and inspire more than any contrived and inappropriate additions. Attentiveness and fidelity to the specific structure of the rite express both a recognition of the nature of Eucharist as a gift and, on the part of the minister, a docile openness to receiving this ineffable gift.[5]

Even as Pope Benedict stressed faithfulness to the rites, he acknowledged that they operate on different levels of communication, engage the whole person, and require a minister's docility. These subjective aspects result from dispositions and style, not just from adherence to rubrics.

Pope Benedict concluded his treatment of *ars celebrandi* with sections on sacred art and liturgical song.[6] Here he moved from his concerns of faithfulness to words and rites back to his opening remarks about beauty and mystery. Many elements make up the "art of proper celebration," including the looks of a building and the sound of its music.

A few years after Pope Benedict's 2007 *Sacramentum Caritatis*, the Vatican promoted another thematic observance, the Year of the Priest. During that year, the Office for the Liturgical Celebrations of the Supreme Pontiff posted "Observance of Liturgical Norms and 'Ars Celebrandi.'"[7] The statement is undated, but the web address assigns it to July 29, 2010. The author is unacknowledged, but the same statement appeared through Zenit news agency a few weeks earlier as a translation of an article in the Spirit of the Liturgy series, written by Father Mauro Gagliardi, a consultor of the same office and professor at the Pontifical Athenaeum Regina Apostolorum in Rome.[8]

Gagliardi claimed general agreement that liturgical abuses increased "in the celebratory field after the Council," and that the recent magisterium called for "the strict observance of the norms." He ad-

[5] *Sacramentum Caritatis*, 40.

[6] *Sacramentum Caritatis*, 41–42.

[7] http://www.vatican.va/news_services/liturgy/details/ns_lit_doc_20100729_osservanza_en.html.

[8] Father Mauro Gagliardi, "Observance of Liturgical Norms and Ars Celebrandi," Zenit (Rome, July 9, 2010), https://www.ewtn.com/catholicism/library/observance-of-liturgical-norms-and-ars-celebrandi-4263.

mitted that liturgical laws are "much more 'open' in relation to the past," yet he alleged that a great number of priests enlarged "the space left to 'creativity'." His examples included the "frequent change of words or whole phrases" in the liturgical books, the insertion of new "rites" foreign to the church's tradition, and inappropriate vestments, vessels and decorations that were sometimes "ridiculous."[9]

For his definition of *ars celebrandi*, Gagliardi wrote, "it does not consist only in the perfect execution of the rites according to the books, but also and above all in the spirit of faith and adoration with which these are celebrated." The *ars celebrandi* "cannot be carried out, however, if it is removed from the norms established for the celebration."[10] Gagliardi thus balanced the "perfect execution" of the rites with a "spirit of faith and adoration." Priests especially bring their personal faith to their liturgical duties. *Ars celebrandi* begins within.

A view balancing precise fulfillment of liturgical laws with personal conduct had emerged in *Eucharisticum Mysterium*, a 1967 instruction on eucharistic worship from the Vatican's Sacred Congregation of Rites.[11] Gagliardi cited it in a footnote: "To foster the correct development of the sacred celebration and the active participation of the faithful, the ministers must not limit themselves to carry out their service with precision, according to the liturgical laws, but they must conduct themselves in such a way as to inculcate, through it, the meaning of sacred things."[12] In the early days after the Council, the Vatican asserted the ineffectiveness of liturgical laws unless they are carried out with meaning.

From the council itself, the Constitution on the Sacred Liturgy stressed the importance of the interior dispositions of all the faithful at worship:

> But in order that the liturgy may be able to produce its full effects it is necessary that the faithful come to it with proper dispositions, that their minds be attuned to their voices, and that they

[9] "Observance of Liturgical Norms," 1.

[10] "Observance of Liturgical Norms," 3.

[11] Sacred Congregation of Rites, *Eucharisticum Mysterium*: Instruction on Eucharistic Worship (May 25, 1967), https://adoremus.org/1967/05/25/eucharisticum-mysterium/.

[12] "Observance of Liturgical Norms," 3, citing *Eucharisticum Mysterium*, 20.

> cooperate with heavenly grace lest they receive it in vain (see 2 Cor 6:1). Pastors of souls must, therefore, realize that, when the liturgy is celebrated, their obligation goes further than simply ensuring that the laws governing valid and lawful celebration are observed. They must also ensure that the faithful take part fully aware of what they are doing, actively engaged in the rite and enriched by it. (SC 11)[13]

Priests' "obligation goes further." For generations, a priest found comfort in the principle that sacraments achieved their effects in themselves, *ex opere operato*, regardless of how personally, sincerely, and accurately he engaged the liturgical rite itself. The council now held priests responsible for helping the people participate meaningfully. The fruitfulness of the liturgy increases with catechetical instruction before worship and artful presiding during it.[14]

The United States Conference of Catholic Bishops (USCCB) described the impact of the priest at the Mass in strong terms:

> No other single factor affects the Liturgy as much as the attitude, style, and bearing of the priest celebrant, who "[prays] in the name of the Church and of the assembled community" (GIRM 33). "When he celebrates the Eucharist, [the priest] must serve God and the people with dignity and humility, and by his bearing and by the way he pronounces the divine words he must convey to the faithful the living presence of Christ" (GIRM 93).[15]

Many Catholics participate better when the priest's obligation goes further than the words and gestures. His attitude, style and bearing all contribute to the art of celebrating.

Different church agencies have thus contributed to a definition of *ars celebrandi*. The Sacred Congregation of Rites asked ministers to

[13] Constitution on the Sacred Liturgy *Sacrosanctum Concilium* [SC] Solemnly Promulgated by His Holiness Pope Paul VI on December 4, 1963. Quotations of Vatican II documents are taken from Austin Flannery, ed., *Vatican Council II: Constitutions, Decrees, Declarations; The Basic Sixteen Documents* (Collegeville, MN: Liturgical Press, 2014).

[14] I am grateful to Bruce Cinquegrani for these insights from his research.

[15] United States Conference of Catholic Bishops, *Sing to the Lord: Music in Divine Worship*, Pastoral Liturgy Series 4 (Washington, DC: United States Conference of Catholic Bishops, 2007), 18.

rely not just on the ceremonies but to inculcate the meaning of sacred things. Pope Benedict expressed the interrelated values of ritual fidelity, the engagement of the whole person, and beauty. The Office for the Liturgical Celebrations of the Supreme Pontiff favored a perfect execution of the rites and a spirit of faith and adoration. The Second Vatican Council solicited the help of priests in engaging the meaningful participation of the faithful. The USCCB appealed to priests to refine their attitude, style and bearing.

Robert Hovda, writing about *ars celebrandi* in the first years after the post–Vatican II liturgical reforms, explored this blend of person and responsibility:

> When one functions as a presider or other minister, it is the whole person, the real person, the true person, the full and complete person who functions. . . .
>
> Of course the personal nature of the presider's presence was always evident in liturgy, but more as a reluctant concession to humanity than as a desirable and valuable gift.[16]

For the sake of this book, I am using the simplest definition of *ars celebrandi*: namely, the art of celebrating. I will argue in favor of both words, not individually, but together. "Celebrating" does indeed imply "proper" celebration. It means an execution of the liturgy according to the liturgical books. Some priests say that they diverge from the books for "pastoral" reasons, often meaning reasons that are "practical" or "personal." One's own subjective judgment of being pastoral is not always a convincing argument for doing something different from what the liturgy provides. Following the liturgical books is a most pastoral thing to do. Even so, a priest's obligation goes further.

"Art" acknowledges that every priest is different. Each brings patterns of speech, distinctive actions, personal faith, and social abilities that affect how he presides. He personally assimilates the signs and symbols of the liturgy that are the church's heritage. Because of individuality, his assimilation of this timeless tradition will be unique. Art is less definable. But it does have good and bad expression. The

[16] Robert W. Hovda, *Strong, Loving and Wise: Presiding in Liturgy* (Collegeville, MN: Liturgical Press, 1976), p. 57.

judgment of good art is subjective, though people can agree on certain principles.

Both words are important. One could precisely celebrate according to the rubrics, though in an artless way. Or, one could use personal artistic gifts that abandon liturgical genius. Good presiding is artful presiding. It is knowledgeable and inspirational. It faithfully grasps the church's heritage and gives it personal expression. It keeps the priest transparent, or, in the words of Father Michael Driscoll, "It seeks to allow Christ to be the artist."[17]

Overview of This Book

This book will apply these principles for artful presiding:

- *Less is more.* In paragraph 40 of *Sacramentum Caritatis,* Pope Benedict promoted the simplicity of gestures and sobriety of signs. This undergirds the artful principle that less is more.
- *Do what it says. Don't do what it doesn't say.* This principle also finds support in paragraph 40, where Pope Benedict dismisses contrived and inappropriate additions to the liturgy. Most priests agree with the first half of this principle, but, whether they lean toward the liturgical left or right, they struggle to apply the second half. The rubrics are neither aimless expressions of self-absorbed authority nor incomplete suggestions inviting impulsive interpretations. They are windows into the deep theological meaning of rituals that unite the universal church in fundamental ways.
- *Offer sacrifice and share communion.* Artful presiding includes spiritual skills such as a strong personal prayer life, a habit of thanksgiving, making sacrifices, and serving the people. It presumes a eucharistic theology consistent with the prayers and rubrics of the Mass, and with the conduct of a priest's life.
- *Be intentional. Eucharisticum Mysterium* says that priests must conduct themselves in ways that inculcate the meaning of sacred things. This is best achieved through intentionality: under-

[17] "The *Ars Celebrandi* and Beauty," *Beyond the Sanctuary: Essays on Liturgy, Life and Discipleship* (Chicago: Liturgy Training Publications, 2020), p. 59.

standing what is being done and executing it with purpose. This applies to words and actions in the liturgy.

- *Involve the people.* Vatican II said that the full, conscious, active participation of the people "is the paramount concern" (SC 14). Artful presiding engages the assembly through the rite and calls forth active participation. This means encouraging the people "to take part by means of acclamations, responses, psalms, antiphons, hymns, as well as by actions, gestures and bodily attitudes" (SC 30). The people thus do not enter a spiritualized "actual" participation, but an intentionally "active" one. As Pope Benedict stated, proper presiding fosters active participation. Proper presiding is more than *celebrandi*. It is also *ars*.

In *Sacramentum Caritatis* Pope Benedict included art and music in the broad areas that contribute to *ars celebrandi*. He has a point. However, this book will focus on the presiding style of the priest.

This book starts with the calendar in order to examine some of the options available to a presider, especially on weekdays. A priest may increase interest in the Mass for himself and for the people if he takes advantage of this variety.

Then it will apply the principles summarized above to the different parts of the Mass. It will treat interactions with other ministers. It will view some frequently overlooked rubrics that could lend more meaning to the celebration.

This section concludes with a few thoughts about how presiding intertwines with other aspects of a priest's ministry. It blends how the priest presides with who the priest is.

The book concludes with a substantial section on concelebration, which proposes an *ars concelebrandi*. After surveying a brief history of concelebration and the theological issues it poses, the book closely examines the rubrics, words, and demeanors of concelebration.

Thank you for giving this book some time when the world is sorting through the effects of a pandemic. You obviously understand that a well-prepared and celebrated liturgy is the church's best response to crisis. No matter on what page of history books they enter the story, priests can always improve the most important work anyone in civilization could ever do: presiding artfully for the celebration of the Mass.

1

Understanding the Calendar

Blending liturgical fidelity with personal gifts begins with the calendar. Some celebrations never move even in a pandemic—such as the Paschal Triduum. Consistently honoring important days demonstrates that individuals belong to a bigger history. The timeless God intervened in time, which the church celebrates at certain sacred times.

Other days, however, carry less significance and come with some freedoms, especially the weekdays of Ordinary Time. *Ars celebrandi* begins when the priest sets his mind on the liturgy at hand. In some cases, he may make surprisingly strong decisions that affect the prayers and readings for the Mass of a particular day.

Solemnities, Feasts, and Memorials

The Universal Norms on the Liturgical Year and Calendar (UNLYC) occupy some of the first pages of the Roman Missal. These norms underwent significant changes with Vatican II. The fruits have affected the dates for observing the memory of certain saints and the ranking of some days above others.

For example, the norms establish the differences among solemnities, feasts, and memorials. Solemnities begin with Evening Prayer I from the Liturgy of the Hours, or vespers of the preceding day. At Mass a solemnity calls for the Gloria and the Creed, even if one falls on a weekday during Lent, such as the Annunciation of the Lord (March 25). The *Lectionary for Mass* generally assigns three Scripture readings and a responsorial psalm for solemnities.

Some solemnities come with their own vigil Mass, such as the Ascension of the Lord, Pentecost Sunday, the Nativity of St. John the Baptist (June 24), Sts. Peter and Paul (June 29), and the Assumption of the Blessed Virgin Mary (August 15). These are to be used at any evening Mass on the preceding day (UNLYC 11). The vigil masses annoy many preachers who want to prepare one homily for the weekend, such as on Pentecost. Nonetheless, the readings for the vigil are to be used. A presider with services on both the vigil and the day may preach more broadly on the theme of the solemnity, solicit the help of another priest or deacon to preach the extra Mass, or prepare two different homilies.

Feasts are celebrated within the natural day, so they have no Evening Prayer I on the preceding night (UNLYC 13). When celebrated at a weekday Mass, feasts call for the Gloria but not the Creed, and the lectionary offers no second reading after the psalm before the gospel. However, Feasts of the Lord form a special category. When one of them falls on a Sunday, the celebration begins on Saturday evening. These include The Presentation of the Lord (February 2), The Transfiguration of the Lord (August 6), The Exaltation of the Holy Cross (September 14), and the Dedication of the Lateran Basilica (November 9). These do include a second reading before the gospel, as well as the Creed on Sundays.

Memorials are obligatory unless they are marked "optional" (UNLYC 14), when the priest may opt in or out of that celebration. Whenever the memorial is observed, the priest must pray its collect, and he may use a preface proper for the day. If a saint's memorial does not include a proper prayer over the offerings or prayer after communion, the priest may select these from the appropriate commons in the following section of the Missal. The Mass for memorials includes neither Gloria nor Creed. Nor does it have a second reading before the gospel.

The Table of Liturgical Days

Immediately following the norms on the calendar near the front of the Missal comes the Table of Liturgical Days. This determines which occasions replace others whenever two occur on the same day. The table is numbered 1 through 13 with many subgroups.

Ranking atop all is the Paschal Triduum of the Passion and Resurrection of the Lord. This will surprise no one except those who insist that Christmas is the best day of the year. Christians participate more personally and consequentially in the paschal mystery than they do in the incarnation.

Christmas ranks atop the days grouped under number 2. However, it shares equal space with the Epiphany, the Ascension, and Pentecost. Others in this grouping are the Sundays of Advent, Lent, and Easter; Ash Wednesday; the weekdays of Holy Week through Thursday morning; and the days within the Octave of Easter.

Then come the solemnities together with All Souls Day, which is kept on a separate line because it does not have all the markers of a solemnity, such as the Gloria, even when it falls on a Sunday.

Number 4 contains a most interesting list of proper solemnities. These are *local* solemnities, rather than global ones. This rank starts with the patron of the place. For example, if a city is named for a saint, that saint's day ranks as a solemnity in the churches within that city.

The next local solemnity is the dedication of a church or the anniversary of its dedication. A church may not be dedicated on any of the days associated with numbers 1-3 on the table. The anniversary becomes a solemnity in that parish every year. If the parish mistakenly does not observe annually the date of its dedication, this needs to be researched and celebrated. It has an impact on the parochial liturgical calendar. The date may be fixed on the anniversary itself, an Ordinary Time Sunday close to the date, or the Sunday before All Saints, "in order to spotlight the bond that links the earthly Church with the heavenly Church." If the date cannot be known, the bishop may assign a date such as the Sunday before November 1 or October 25.[1]

The title of the parish church also ranks as a solemnity. For example, if the building was dedicated to St. Munchin, who does not even appear on the universal liturgical calendar, then January 2 becomes a solemnity in that parish, replacing the local observance of Sts. Basil the Great and Gregory Nazianzen, because the Roman Martyrology also assigns January 2 to St. Munchin. If through a

[1] *"Documentorum Explanatio: De Celebratione Annuali Dedicationis Ecclesiae," Notitiae* 8 71/3 (March 1972): 103.

restructuring process a combined parish receives a new name, the title of the church cannot be changed, and the date associated with the church's original title remains a solemnity in that parish, whose new patron is celebrated as a feast.[2]

A parish may celebrate its titular day or anniversary of dedication on a Sunday in Ordinary Time when the actual day falls on a weekday. In fact, any day of special interest to the people may be observed on a Sunday in Ordinary Time as long as it ranks at numbers 4 or 5 in the Table of Liturgical Days (UNLYC 58). Usually it is moved to the Sunday before or after, and that seems to be the intent of this permission. But it does not exclude another nearby Sunday.

Numbers 5 and 6 show the ranking of Feasts "of the Lord" above the Sundays in Ordinary Time, which explains why, for example, the Transfiguration is observed on August 6 every year, even when it falls on a Sunday. Other feasts on the general calendar occupy level 7.

Number 8 lists proper feasts; that is, those pertaining to the local church, not the universal church. These include the principal patron of the diocese and the patron of a parish if different from the title of the parish church.

The anniversary of the dedication of the cathedral, a solemnity in the cathedral itself, is observed as a *feast* throughout the rest of the diocese. Every parish has the *cathedral's* anniversary of dedication on its annual calendar. The priest uses the presidential prayers from the commons for the dedication of a church, and the readings come from the same section of the lectionary. Mass that day includes the Gloria, even if it falls on a weekday in Advent or Lent. If the cathedral's anniversary date lands on a Sunday in Ordinary Time, it is observed only at the cathedral that year. If the dedication anniversary falls on any day that ranks above number 4, even a weekday in Holy Week, then the cathedral observes its solemnity on the next available date, but the parishes do not observe the feast that year.

The weekdays of Lent are at number 9, just below the weekdays from December 17–24 and the days within the octave of Christmas.

[2] Table of Liturgical Days, 8e; Sacred Congregation for Divine Worship, *Patronus, Liturgica Acceptione*, "On Patron Saints," March 19, 1973, 3a, in International Commission on English in the Liturgy (ICEL), *Documents on the Liturgy, 1963–1979: Conciliar, Papal, and Curial Texts*, ed. and trans. Thomas C. O'Brien (Collegeville, MN: Liturgical Press, 1982), 477.

Obligatory memorials come at number 10—below the weekdays of Lent. If an obligatory memorial falls during Lent, it becomes a commemoration, meaning it is optional, not obligatory, and of all the Mass parts normally associated with the memorial, only its collect may be used.

More days of lesser rank round out the calendar, and the very last entry under number 13 specifies the weekdays in Ordinary Time. They are the least powerful of all the days on the calendar.

Ordinary Time Weekdays

A priest may choose from an array of Mass texts on weekdays in Ordinary Time. The art of celebrating may first arise here. He may choose a saint's day, a Mass for various needs, a votive Mass, or a Mass for the dead. Because optional memorials are indeed optional, the same flexibility applies on days assigned to them.

The Catholic Church's complete listing of saints is found in the Roman Martyrology, which arranges them in calendar order. Any given day lists a dozen or fewer or many more saints. The martyrology has been updated twice since Vatican II, but the English translation is not yet available. The number of canonized saints increases each year, so modifications to the martyrology happen frequently. Therefore, on a day like September 5, even though Mother Teresa of Calcutta may not appear in the Missal of a given episcopal conference, any priest may celebrate her memorial on that day, as long as it falls on a weekday in Ordinary Time.

The Missal's Masses and Prayers for Various Needs and Occasions contains a treasure for ecclesial, civic, or personal occasions. The collects may even be used outside of Mass for gatherings of committees or parish groups. Many times the readings assigned to a particular weekday in Ordinary Time resonate with themes from one of these masses. The priest may use these prayers in harmony with the word of God that day. On an obligatory memorial, if "some real necessity or pastoral advantage calls for it," one of these Masses may replace the memorial (GIRM 376).

Votive Masses offer presidential prayers with devotional themes such as the Most Holy Trinity, the Sacred Heart of Jesus, the Blessed

Virgin Mary, and the Saints. On a weekday in Ordinary Time, the priest may choose one of these masses. As with the previous category, if some necessity or advantage calls for it, he may use one of these sets in place of an obligatory memorial.

Masses for the Dead may be celebrated on weekdays in Ordinary Time or on optional memorials. However, the priest does not have the freedom to replace an obligatory memorial with a Mass for the Dead, probably to put aside the former custom of celebrating these on nearly every available weekday. By exception, he may celebrate one of the Masses for the Dead on receiving the news of a death, for the final burial, or the first anniversary, all of which are permitted on memorials and on weekdays of Ordinary Time, Christmas, Lent and Easter, except on Ash Wednesday or during Holy Week (GIRM 381). The prayers for an anniversary are in the Missal's Masses for the Dead, part II, and the others draw from part III, "Various Commemorations" for one or more deceased persons.

Once again, perhaps based on the readings or some pertinent event in parish or social life, the priest may substitute the daily Mass prayers with any of these options.

The weekday readings are preferred. Each of these categories of Masses in the Missal come with corresponding readings in the Lectionary. On any saint's day, the Lectionary suggests readings that pertain to the life of that saint. These were chosen with great care but are to be used sparingly. "The Priest will take care not to omit too frequently and without sufficient reason the readings assigned each day in the Lectionary to the weekdays, for the Church desires that a richer portion at the table of God's Word should be spread before the people" (GIRM 355c). By sustaining the weekday readings, the presider helps the people appreciate a given day's readings within the scope of those assigned for the week.

For vestment color, the priest may wear green or the color associated with the Mass he has chosen to celebrate—red for martyrs or a votive Mass for the Holy Spirit; purple for a Mass of repentance, for example. Ordinary Time weekday celebrations can maintain a balance of uniformity and diversity when the vesture is green, the assigned readings are proclaimed, but the presider explores the variety of collects, exposing participants to the wealth of prayers within the Missal.

Weddings and Funerals

The Order of Celebrating Matrimony (OCM) says that the ritual Mass "For the Celebration of Marriage" may be used on any day except on numbers 1 through 4 in the Table of Liturgical Days (34). Weddings may take place either outside of Mass or within a different Mass on those days. For example, if someone requests a wedding Mass on a Saturday night in Ordinary Time, the presider may use the prayers and readings from the ritual Mass for matrimony because Sundays in Ordinary Time rank at number 6 on the table, well below the excluded areas. But if the couple want a wedding Mass on a Saturday night in Easter Time, they may have a wedding, and it may take place during a special Mass, but the priest is to use the presidential prayers and readings for that Sunday. The same applies to the Saturday evenings and Sundays of Advent and Lent.

The same also applies to the anniversary of the dedication of the church where the couple plan to get married. In fact, both the church's titular day and anniversary day come under number 4 on the Table of Liturgical Days. If one of those falls on a Saturday, for example, a morning wedding Mass that day is celebrated within the larger celebration of the history of that church: The readings and presidential prayers of the solemnity apply to the Mass used for the wedding. The same applies to a Saturday night wedding Mass in Ordinary Time if one of these solemnities should fall on the Sunday. If the wedding takes place without Mass, however, all the readings and prayers come from the appropriate section of the OCM, no matter the liturgical day.

Funerals are another matter. A funeral without Mass may take place on any day. A funeral with Mass may take place on any day except holydays of obligation, the Triduum (including Holy Thursday morning), and Sundays of Advent, Lent, and Easter (GIRM 380). Unlike matrimony, where a Saturday night wedding could take place inside a Lent Sunday Mass, a funeral may not. Funerals may take place at a Sunday Mass only in Ordinary Time.

This comes up more commonly on holydays of obligation. If someone requests a funeral Mass on November 1 (All Saints) or December 8 (The Immaculate Conception of the Blessed Virgin Mary), it cannot be done. Only a funeral without Mass is permitted on those days.

The implication is that the family is expected to participate in a holyday Mass the same day. Few may be able to do that. A pastor has the authority to dispense them from that obligation.[3] This is one occasion when that may prove helpful.

The Eucharistic Prayers

Another way to add variety and precision to the art of presiding is through the choice of the eucharistic prayer. The Catholic liturgy offers ten of these. Four appear within the Order of Mass (OM), three in its appendix, and three of them are not in the Missal at all, but all of them may be used.

Eucharistic Prayer I is the venerable Roman Canon. The earliest record of it comes from St. Ambrose near the end of the fourth century. Versions over the next few centuries nearly doubled its length. The liturgical renewal after Vatican II made some minor changes to it: Some internal concluding phrases became optional, many signs of the cross disappeared, and the imposition of hands moved to a different section, for example. The post–Vatican II Missal also made some alterations to the institution narrative and consecration, a change of greater import. But overall, it remains the same Roman Canon.

Although there are nine other eucharistic prayers, this one may always be used (GIRM 365a). Many priests have strong opinions about the Roman Canon. Some never touch it; others use it exclusively.

The GIRM recommends Eucharistic Prayer I for occasions that call for special intercessions (GIRM 365a). For example, the section that begins, "In communion with those whose memory we venerate" receives a pertinent gloss on certain days in the liturgical year: Christmas and its octave, the Epiphany, the Easter Vigil and its octave, the Ascension, and Pentecost. These variations appear right within the Order of Mass, most accessible to the presider.

Other insertions appear on occasions when certain rituals are celebrated. These affect the sections that begin, "Remember, Lord, your

[3] Code of Canon Law, 1245.

servants," and "Therefore, Lord, we pray." The insertions are harder to find, but an artful celebrant becomes familiar with them. The Missal gathers its ritual Masses in the back third of the book, with insertions for the scrutinies, the conferral of baptism, the conferral of confirmation, and the celebration of marriage, for example.

The GIRM also recommends Eucharistic Prayer I on celebrations of the Apostles and Saints mentioned in it (GIRM 365a). These include the days assigned to Sts. Peter and Paul (June 29), Felicity and Perpetua (February 7), and Cecilia (November 22). The GIRM does not require a priest to use the Roman Canon on any of these liturgical days or sacramental occasions, but it finds this prayer especially suited for them.

The Roman Canon has no preface of its own. It never did. The priest has always selected a preface from among those available for the day. Although the pre–Vatican II Missal contained only a few prefaces, the post–Vatican II Missal blossomed with dozens more. Whenever a single preface is not assigned for the day, part of the *ars celebrandi* is selecting a preface that best fits the occasion at hand. Such choices may enhance the use of Eucharistic Prayer I.

Eucharistic Prayer II has probably become the most popular eucharistic prayer because it is the shortest of the ten. The compilers of the post–Vatican II Missal believed it shared the Roman Canon's place and age of composition.

It is recommended for weekdays and for "special circumstances," though it is unclear what those may be (GIRM 365b). Eucharistic Prayer II comes with its own preface based on the opening words of its earliest version. The priest is not bound to it, however; he may replace it with another preface appropriate for the day's celebration, as Eucharist Prayer I forces him to do. Even so, the GIRM makes two easily overlooked suggestions: It recommends a preface that sums up the mystery of salvation, probably because the prayer's original preface did; and it points the priest toward the common prefaces, probably hoping that on more solemn days with a special preface he would avoid using Eucharistic Prayer II (GIRM 365b).

Several of the ritual Masses, however, which can be days of great solemnity, call for interpolations in Prayer II, just as Eucharistic Prayer I does. These include the scrutinies, the conferral of baptism, the conferral of confirmation, and the celebration of marriage. Located in the back of the Missal, these are best marked with a ribbon before Mass begins.

In Masses for a particular deceased person—more than those for all the dead—Eucharistic Prayer II makes a good choice because the priest may include the special insert for the dead, which more conveniently appears on the same pages in the Missal with the rest of the prayer. Commonly a priest uses this insert at funeral Masses, but he may say it in the Mass on receiving the news of a death, for the final burial, or the first anniversary. Again, these Masses, found in parts II and III of the Missal's Masses for the Dead, are set aside on those certain weekdays when the community grieves the loss of one member (GIRM 380).

Eucharistic Prayer III was newly composed after Vatican II as one of its fruits. It is "preferred on Sundays and festive days" (GIRM 365c). For funerals or for any Mass for the Dead, the priest may add the special formula for the deceased person located within its pages near the end of the prayer.

Prayer III especially serves as an alternative to Prayer I. It comes without a specific preface, causing the priest to select a most appropriate one. Its streamlined structure and direct language speak more clearly to many congregations. It is shorter than Prayer I, making it more accessible to many as well. It feels grander than Prayer II, simply because of its more generous length.

Eucharistic Prayer IV was also composed after Vatican II, though it relies on ancient models such as the Anaphora of St. Basil. Prayer IV has an invariable preface. The reason is easier to see in the 2011 revised English translation than it was before. The preface praises God for the creation of the earth and the angels, and then after the *Sanctus* the prayer turns to the creation of human beings.

The uses for Prayer IV are therefore somewhat limited. For example, it does not include an insertion for Masses for the Dead because the priest cannot substitute this prayer's preface with any other one. This discourages its use from occasions such as a funeral. At Masses for the Dead, Prayers I through III make a better choice.

Prayer IV is long, and some priests therefore limit its use. Still, it has lovely moments. The biblically literate spot dozens of references to favorite passages throughout. Chockfull of such allusions, Prayer IV serves as the most scripturally rich text of all ten eucharistic prayers.

The Missal places the Eucharistic Prayer for Use in Masses for Various Needs in an appendix to the Order of Mass. This was a historical decision, not a theological one. A revised Order of Mass crystallized after Vatican II, but then the Missal received new content. This prayer has as much efficacy as any other eucharistic prayer. It just occupies less prime territory. It was developed as a product of the Swiss synod of bishops. Because the word "synod" comes from the two Greek words for "journey together," *hodos* and *syn*, the image of journeying appears frequently in this prayer.

It is marked with roman numeral V (5), numbering it as the fifth eucharistic prayer. It has four iterations, marked accordingly. Although some people assume that it is therefore four distinct eucharistic prayers, the Missal considers it as one prayer with four versions. It is "appropriately used" on those weekdays when the priest offers the presidential prayers for a Mass for Various Needs and Occasions.[4] Although not explicitly excluded from Sunday celebrations, this eucharistic prayer was not created for them, except for the instances when a bishop replaces an Ordinary Time liturgy with one of these Masses.[5] The prefaces are invariable.[6]

The titles of the four versions articulate their purpose, and the headings recommend uses for each prayer. The first, "The Church on the Path of Unity," is fitting for Masses For the Church, For the Pope, For the Bishop, For the Election of a Pope or a Bishop, For a Council or Synod, For Priests, For the Priest Himself, For Ministers of the Church, and For a Spiritual or Pastoral Gathering. It applies well whenever the universal or the local church has special needs.

The second, "God Guides His Church along the Way of Salvation," is suggested For the Church, For Vocations to Holy Orders, For the Laity, For the Family, For Religious, For Vocations to Religious Life, For Charity, For Relatives and Friends, and For Giving Thanks to God. It pertains well for occasions that support the everyday expression of discipleship.

[4] Roman Missal, Eucharistic Prayer for Use in Masses for Various Needs, 1.

[5] Roman Missal, Masses and Prayers for Various Needs and Occasions, 2.

[6] In the Missal, the paragraph introducing the Eucharistic Prayers for Reconciliation explicitly permits the substitution of its prefaces with others that refer to penance and conversion, but the introduction to the Eucharistic Prayers for Various Needs and Occasions does not offer the same permission.

The third, "Jesus, the Way to the Father," works especially well with Masses For the Evangelization of Peoples, For Persecuted Christians, For the Nation or State, For Those in Public Office, For a Governing Assembly, At the Beginning of the Civil Year, and For the Progress of Peoples. It carries a message of evangelization.

The fourth, "Jesus, Who Went About Doing Good," is appropriate for Masses For Refugees and Exiles, In Time of Famine or For Those Suffering Hunger, For Our Oppressors, For Those Held in Captivity, For Those in Prison, For the Sick, For the Dying, For the Grace of a Happy Death, and In Any Need. At first, the title seems like faint praise for the person and ministry of Jesus, but it alludes to part of the catechesis that Peter gave the household of Cornelius in Acts 10:38. This version of the prayer inspires outreach to those on the margins.

The same appendix to the Order of Mass includes two Eucharistic Prayers for Reconciliation. Pope Paul VI authorized these for a holy year on the theme of reconciliation in 1975. The Missal recommends them for Masses for Promoting Harmony, For Reconciliation, For the Preservation of Peace and Justice, In Time of War or Civil Disturbance, For the Forgiveness of Sins, For Charity, of the Mystery of the Holy Cross, of the Most Holy Eucharist, of the Most Precious Blood of our Lord Jesus Christ, as well as in Masses during Lent. Although each of them comes with a preface consonant with its theme, other prefaces that deal with penance and conversion may be used. Some priests like the first one during Advent and the second during Lent with the appropriate seasonal prefaces, but the Missal gives more freedom. It benefits the people of God to hear them on occasions when the readings and homily carry a penitential theme.

The Eucharistic Prayers for Masses with Children exist in a volume separate from the Missal. They did not go through the entire process of retranslation. They were simply fluffed up a bit with necessary changes such as the revised preface dialogue and institution narrative, and then set back into use.

These prayers reside outside the vernacular Missal because the Missal in Latin excluded them—with good reason. They are the only prayers in the entire Missal that may not be prayed in Latin. They were composed for the better comprehension of children, so they must be offered in the vernacular languages. Because the vernacular Missals are to translate the Latin Missal as closely as possible, the

Vatican excluded these prayers from the English Missal and authorized their publication only in a separate fascicle.

As these were being composed, the first two in French and the third in German, the authors had in mind different age groups of children. Prayers I through III originally moved from the youngest congregation to the oldest. The Vatican eliminated these age distinctions when it first published the prayers, but one can still detect the authors' intent. A priest offers these only with any large group of preadolescent children.

In summary, here are some recommendations for the artful selection of eucharistic prayers.

Eucharistic Prayer I works well on all the recommended days—those with a special seasonal insert and those that celebrate one of the saints it mentions. It fits a few other occasions as well, such as the First Martyrs of the Holy Roman Church (June 30) and the Dedication of the Lateran Basilica (November 9), because both of these days pertain to the city associated with the composition of the prayer; as well as the memorial of St. Ambrose (December 7), whose writings gave us the earliest evidence of the Roman Canon.

For an obscure reason, Prayer I could fittingly be used on the Thirty-First Sunday in Ordinary Time. One of the sources for the Roman Canon is the seventh-century Gelasian Sacramentary, where the entire prayer seemingly haphazardly appears among the texts of one particular Mass near the end of the collection. The prayer after communion for that day in the Gelasian now appears in the Roman Missal on the Thirty-First Sunday in Ordinary Time. In homage to the history of the Roman Canon, one could pray it on the same day with the prayer after communion that served as its companion long, long ago.

Eucharistic Prayer II is the go-to prayer for weekdays. It may be used on Sundays for the sake of varying the prayers, but occasionally, rather than regularly. Some priests use it simply to speed up the Mass, which is never a good reason. If offered sparingly in Ordinary Time, Prayer II's appearance in Advent, for example, may convey a sense of simplicity. Prayer II would be fitting for the optional memorial of St. Hippolytus on August 13. At the time of the council, scholars thought that Hippolytus had authored the prayer. Now it seems most likely that he did not, though his association with Prayer II lingers.

Eucharistic Prayer III works well on Sundays and solemnities. It clearly and grandly articulates the faith of the church. Its space for an applicable preface makes it completely flexible for all occasions. Its use on feasts lends more gravity to a weekday liturgy.

Eucharistic Prayer IV deserves rotation throughout Ordinary Time, both on Sundays and on weekdays. Practically, it may receive special attention on Sundays a couple of weeks before Lent and before the Solemnity of Christ the King of the Universe because the priest sets it aside during Advent and Christmas, Lent and Easter. Similarly, the return to Ordinary Time may signal an appropriate occasion to reintroduce the community to Eucharistic Prayer IV.

The Eucharistic Prayer for Use in Masses for Various Needs applies especially to the weekdays in Ordinary Time when the priest offers one of the pertinent Masses. He judiciously chooses the occasions for the Eucharistic Prayers for Reconciliation, which receive considerable favor during Lent on Sundays and weekdays.

With a congregation of preadolescent children, the eucharistic prayers designed for the occasion help keep them engaged. These prayers improve with the association of musicians, who can enliven the children's many acclamations.

Each priest probably likes some eucharistic prayers better than others. Many Catholics do too. A thoughtful *ars celebrandi* uses all the eucharistic prayers for the sake of precision and diversity. People deserve to hear the prayers that some priests rarely say. Priests serve the people well when they grow comfortable with all ten. Some eucharistic prayers may not be a priest's personal favorites, but if he offers a prayer well, the people will come to love it even more. All ten give thanks to God and obtain the manifold gifts of the Holy Spirit.

2

Presiding: Grounding Principles

The Marriage of Books and Ministers

The introduction to this book highlights these principles for an *ars celebrandi*: Less is more. Do what it says; don't do what it doesn't say. Offer sacrifice and share communion. Be intentional. Involve the people.

All of these involve a marriage of books and ministers. The liturgical norms encounter a real-time relationship with the individual persons ordained to carry them out. Like many marriages, this one is complicated.

The relationship presumes that priests know the liturgical norms. However, the rules are complex. The books detailing them are many. Some laws keep changing. Consequently, a priest may not be following liturgical rules simply because he does not completely understand them. The same applies to fields such as the Code of Canon Law. Those who want to abide by the rules may not have mastered them all.

Furthermore, not every aspect of liturgy is prescribed. When presiding, a typical priest is supposed to do certain things, is free to do certain other things, and *takes* freedom to do even more. Some priests say, "I do the red and say the black." They mean that they do the rubrics and say the words as both are printed in the liturgical books.

But they probably don't. Virtually every priest does something that is not quite prescribed in the book, even bishops, even popes.

Take the question of preconciliar rubrics. Some priests wear the maniple, use a burse, limit the extension of their hands, press their canonical digits after the consecration, make a sign of the cross with the host before receiving or giving communion, and add swings of the censer. All those practices have been discontinued.

Some priests add devotional prayers such as the Hail Mary, which was never part of the Mass, or the Prayer to St. Michael, which was discontinued in 1969. The universal prayer was designed to cover contemporary needs with explicit intentions that could legitimately implore the aid of saints.

When Pope Benedict extended the usage of what he named the extraordinary form of the liturgy, he signed an accompanying letter to bishops. He wrote that "the two Forms of the usage of the Roman Rite can be mutually enriching: new Saints and some of the new Prefaces can and should be inserted in the old Missal." He promoted the sacrality of celebration in the post–Vatican II Missal of Paul VI. He said the "most sure guarantee" of the present Missal's ability to unite and be loved by parish communities is to celebrate it "with great reverence in harmony with the liturgical directives."[1] Although Pope Benedict called for a mutual enrichment, he proposed that the former Missal adopt parts of the current Missal, and that those using the current Missal be faithful to it. His letter by itself did not explicitly promote or permit the insertion of preconciliar rubrics into the Missal of Paul VI.

So, one principle of *ars celebrandi* cuts both ways: Do what it says; don't do what it doesn't say. Whether a priest adopts a casual interpretation of rubrics or restores abandoned ones, he is doing what it does not say. That opens the door to principles difficult to defend: "It used to be done this way." "I like it this way." "It's more reverent this way." "It's more pastoral this way."

[1] Letter of His Holiness Benedict XVI to the Bishops on the Occasion of the Publication of the Apostolic Letter "motu proprio data" *Summorum Pontificum* on the Use of the Roman Liturgy Prior to the Reform of 1970 (July 7, 2007), http://www.vatican.va/content/benedict-xvi/en/letters/2007/documents/hf_ben-xvi_let_20070707_lettera-vescovi.html.

Less is more. By not doing what it does not say, a priest uncovers the meaning of what it does say. If he puts his energies into the words and actions of the Missal and restrains himself from adding more, he encounters the deeper meaning of the Missal of Paul VI.

The liturgical experts who worked on the Missal in the 1960s made difficult but wise decisions to shape a celebration of the Eucharist that emphasized the participation of the people in a living exercise of their baptismal priesthood. The Mass doesn't need any fixing. If people leave it alone, it will be just fine.

The Question of *Ad Orientem*

For the Liturgy of the Eucharist the priest presides at a freestanding altar, and he faces the people. Some people like the preconciliar practice in which the altar abuts the back wall of the church, and the priest offers the eucharistic prayer with his back to the people. That posture is sometimes called facing *ad orientem*, or "toward the East," because churches traditionally orient on an axis that puts the altar at the east end. Even if the church faces a different way, the side with the altar may be called "liturgical east." The rubrics, however, prefer that the priest face the people.[2]

Most significantly, GIRM 299 says, "The altar should be built separate from the wall, in such a way that it is possible to walk around it easily and that Mass can be celebrated at it facing the people, which is desirable wherever possible." The same paragraph says that "the altar should occupy a place where it is truly the center toward which the attention of the whole congregation of the faithful naturally turns." These rules are repeated in the *Order of Dedication of a Church and an Altar*; this ensures that newly dedicated altars are freestanding so that the priest may face the congregation (IV:8). The GIRM calls this piece of furniture both altar and table (296), which is easily discerned when it is detached from the wall, gathering people around.

Even the presider's chair is to face the people. It may suitably occupy the area at the head of the sanctuary, where the altar formerly

[2] What follows is a condensation of my article, "The Amen Corner: About Face," *Worship* 90 (November 2016): 484–91.

stood, unless the tabernacle has been placed there. The GIRM refers to the area "behind the altar," meaning that the altar stands apart from the wall (GIRM 310). The ambo too is placed where those who use it look at the people (GIRM 309, 133, 138). Whereas the preconciliar liturgy put both parts of the Mass at the altar against the wall, the postconciliar reform positions the priest where he faces the people throughout.

Many have observed, however, that the Missal instructs both priest and deacon when to face the people, as if this implies that presiding *ad orientem* is an equal option. It is not. These indications tell the clergy how to preside at historical altars that offer no alternative. "Wherever possible" (GIRM 299), the priest should face the people. Consequently, the instructions from the Missal cover exceptional circumstances where the clergy absolutely need to face the people at certain times. In the introductory rites, this happens at the sign of the cross (OM 1) and the greeting (GIRM 124). Because the ambo is positioned where a person reading the intercessions faces the people (GIRM 138), the deacon or priest also looks at them for the greeting before the gospel. This was not the case in the preconciliar liturgy, where both greeting and gospel were said *ad orientem*. At the preparation of the gifts, the priest faces the people to invite their prayer (OM 29 and GIRM 146). The deacon or priest faces them to initiate the sign of peace (OM 127 and GIRM 154). When proclaiming "Behold the Lamb of God," the priest again faces the people (OM 132 and GIRM 157). For the concluding rites he looks at the people to greet them (OM 141). For the dismissal the deacon or priest faces the people (OM 144). Clearly, the point is to have the priest or deacon face the people for the sake of dialogues that involve them. Even in preconciliar churches that have never had a freestanding altar, the postconciliar liturgy has them face the people at these times.

These postconciliar rubrics do not tell the priest or deacon to turn away from the people when the dialogue concludes. In normal circumstances, they always face the people and need not turn at all. In exceptional circumstances, they will naturally turn back to the altar to continue reading from the Missal. The postconciliar Missal's clearest indication for the priest to face the altar is for his reception of communion (OM 33 and GIRM 158, 244, and 268). If he has had to turn in order to face the people for "Behold the Lamb of God," he must face the altar to consume the host. This protects the host in the unlikely event that he drops it while placing it in his mouth.

Other liturgies of the Roman Rite concur with these directives, especially during Holy Week. At the Chrism Mass, if the oil of the sick is blessed during the eucharistic prayer, the ministers who carry the vessel bring it to the altar and hold it in front of the bishop.[3] This would be impossible if he were not facing the people across the altar. To bless the oil of catechumens, the bishop faces the people.[4] In the preconciliar liturgy, he sat on a faldstool and faced the altar.

On Good Friday the priest says the opening prayer facing the people.[5] He has not made the sign of the cross or greeted the people as usual, so the rubrics explain that he faces them for the prayer. Because his chair is to face the people, this is the usual position even for the collect at Mass. When the priest receives the cross on Good Friday, he faces the people.[6] When the deacon leads the dialogue concerning the light of Christ at the Easter Vigil, he faces the people before setting the candle in its stand.[7]

At weddings the priest has always faced the couple during the nuptial blessing, even before the council, and even though he addresses God. At the funeral of a priest, his coffin is traditionally placed in the center aisle in the opposite direction from the funeral of a lay Catholic, so that even in death he occupies the position he held at every Eucharist: facing the people.

All these examples show the reverence the church has for the prayers that the priest addresses to God while facing the people. The rubrics have a clear expectation that celebrating *ad orientem* is not an equal option. As this book notes, however, "facing the people" is not the same as "looking at the people." When the priest prays, he will help the people pray if he looks above them rather than at them.

[3] *The Order of Blessing the Oil of Catechumens and of the Sick and of Consecrating the Chrism*, 20.

[4] *Order of Blessing the* Oil, 22.

[5] Roman Missal, Friday of the Passion of the Lord, 6.

[6] Roman Missal, Friday of the Passion of the Lord, 15.

[7] Roman Missal, The Easter Vigil in the Holy Night, 17.

Styles

Each priest celebrates Mass in his personal style. He uses his gifts to preside effectively for the assembly. Even though all priests use the same liturgical books, they embody the liturgy in unique ways. Hovda states simply, "Good style in liturgy is appropriate, honest, authentic, as real and genuine as it can be."[8]

If less is more, a good presider tries not to add unnecessary words. He becomes as transparent as possible, letting the words of the Missal lead the way.

Priests are celebrants, not celebrities. People can learn sports scores and weather reports in other ways. Pope Francis wrote about the homily, "Nor is it fitting to talk about the latest news in order to awaken people's interest; we have television programmes for that."[9] The same can be said of the way priests greet the people at the start of the liturgy. They best avoid calling attention to themselves. Admittedly, people often do treat priests like celebrities. Priests' names and faces are well known. But at Mass priests are servants of the liturgy, not of their own ego.

A priest's unique styles will be effective if he discerns his gifts and uses them properly. He has a duty to the church's liturgy and to the people gathered to celebrate it. A good *ars celebrandi* weighs his own preferences against those of the people of God. They have a right to the liturgy in which they are called to participate.

This requires some humility on the part of the priest. Some priests establish parish customs that they think will last for generations to come. Then when the bishop reassigns them, a new pastor may change some of the "traditions" they assumed would last forever. In extreme cases, liturgical whiplash spiritually maltreats the people of God.

[8] Robert W. Hovda, *Strong, Loving and Wise: Presiding in Liturgy* (Collegeville, MN: Liturgical Press, 1976), p. 63.

[9] Apostolic Exhortation *Evangelii Gaudium* of the Holy Father Francis to the Bishops, Clergy, Consecrated Persons and the Lay Faithful on the Proclamation of the Gospel in Today's World (November 24, 2013), http://www.vatican.va/content/francesco/en/apost_exhortations/documents/papa-francesco_esortazione-ap_20131124_evangelii-gaudium.html, 155.

Even without a change in pastor, people experience a variety of presiders in different venues more than priests typically do. Many people know better than priests how presiding styles and actions differ. The priest who makes a decision because it is "pastoral" or "traditional" may need to check that he hasn't masked a preference that is actually "personal." If he has, it does not serve the people.

A priest who cultivates his style, his *ars celebrandi*, makes a happy marriage between his personal gifts and the liturgical norms he serves.

Progressive Solemnity

Not all celebrations are alike. Even when the same people gather in the same building, different occasions call for grades of solemnity.

The principle of "progressive solemnity" first appeared in the 1967 instruction *Musicam Sacram* from the Vatican's Sacred Congregation of Rites. It referred to music for the Liturgy of the Hours.[10] In context, it applied to singing some parts of the office, while reciting other parts. In principle, it implies that a more solemn event would call for more singing.

The principle can be applied in other ways. Not just music, but the use of incense, the choice of vestments, the length of processions, and the number of candles can all help people sense the relative solemnity of the occasion. People make similar appraisals in daily life. How they dress, for example, indicates their interpretation of the relative solemnity of the occasion at hand.

Buildings themselves influence the quality of worship within them. Some buildings, grand in design, foster a more formal celebration of the liturgy than other buildings, more immediate in their design. Worship can happen in any building. Often the building predetermines the effectiveness of the styles people employ within them.

In some parishes, ethnicity plays a strong role in expressions of solemnity. Forms of dress, sounds of music, and extent of gestures will all differ from one community to another. What is formal in one

[10] *Musicam Sacram* Instruction on Music in the Liturgy (March 5, 1967), http://www.vatican.va/archive/hist_councils/ii_vatican_council/documents/vat-ii_instr_19670305_musicam-sacram_en.html, 38.

place may be informal in another. A priest who experiences these different environments learns that solemnity is supple.

Whether liturgical celebrations are solemn or less formal, they serve best when they keep the attention on God, not on the priest.

3

Intentionality in Act

One priest tells a story of his mother, who enjoyed gambling at local casinos. She showed up so often at the boats that everyone knew her as The Captain. One day she invited her son home for lunch and opened the conversation with this question: "Do you know the difference between praying at the boats and praying in church?" The priest smiled at this pseudo-theological question coming from his own mother's lips. He followed the conversation to its logical conclusion. "No, what is the difference between praying at the boats and praying in church?" She squared her silverware, leaned in toward him at the table, looked him in the eye, and in all sincerity declared, "When you pray at the boats, you really mean it."

The people of God can tell whether or not a priest means the prayers he says at Mass. Some priests clip through the words without much thought. If they have not made the prayer their own, they diminish the same possibility for the people.

Hovda underscored the essentialness of a presider's depth and commitment of faith:

> It suggests personal belief that is real and meaningful and operative, and a disposition to prayer, especially prayer of praise and thanksgiving. . . . These qualities are closely bound up with feelings of awe, mystery, the holy, reverence, which simply have

> to be present in the one who presides in liturgical celebration. . . . The best presiding techniques appear shrill, pretentious, self-assertive and empty without this qualification. The worst techniques are made bearable (if not delectable) by its presence.[1]

Intentionality applies not just to words, but to actions and even to the way a priest uses his body.

Using the Body

Intentionality begins with appropriate vestments. The amice and cincture are optional, and are worn if needed to conceal "ordinary clothing at the neck" (GIRM 336, cf. 119) and to cinch up an overly long alb. The appropriate color of vestments applies to the stole and chasuble. Vestments come in a variety of styles because the Mass has crossed many centuries. A dignified and beautiful vestment that blends with the liturgical space could be ancient or modern. By contrast, the poor design or condition of some vestments may distract people. An appropriate vestment fits the priest—neither so short that it calls attention to his trousers, nor so long that it threatens to trip him.

When vesting, an intentional presider removes his watch. Mass unfolds in its own time ungoverned by the clock. A priest who wears a watch during Mass will likely check it multiple times. That will distract him as well as the people at prayer. By not wearing a watch, a priest shows that nothing else could possibly be more important than the Eucharist he is celebrating.

Some priests recite the discontinued preconciliar prayers to accompany the donning of vestments. The practice seems harmless enough, and many priests find that the prayerful placement of vestments helps intentionality. Some priests still kiss the stole before putting it on, even though the rubrics do not call for it. Following the principle, "Do what it says; don't do what it does not say," a priest may find that by not kissing the stole, the kisses he gives the altar and the book of the gospels stand out in greater relief. Less is more.

[1] Hovda, *Strong, Loving and Wise*, p. 13.

The prescribed kisses show affection for the community's two primary symbols of Christ in the two main parts of the Mass: the Liturgy of the Word and of the Eucharist.

Some priests wear the stole over the chasuble, a practice that gained some traction in the years after Vatican II though without any formal approval. It may have evolved from the pursuit of greater variety in the liturgy, or as a plainer visual distinction from a deacon, whose dalmatic more closely resembles a chasuble to the casual observer, but whose stole looks really different. The Missal simply states that the chasuble is worn over the stole "unless otherwise indicated" (GIRM 337). Although a deacon may omit the dalmatic "out of necessity or on account of a lesser degree of solemnity" (GIRM 119) the presider always wears a chasuble.

Many priests vest well before Mass begins, move from sacristy to vestibule, and greet people as they enter. Another possibility is to greet parishioners only before vesting. No rubric governs this decision. By design, though, the vestments are liturgical. If greeting parishioners in a clergy suit, a priest is freer to write notes about the information people share: their names, their milestones, the sick and the dead among their families and friends, their children's catechesis, their requests for an appointment, or a blessing of their home. After a time of visiting, and just before Mass begins, a priest may put on the sacred vestments that befit the liturgical duties he then starts to fulfill.

After vesting, a wise priest looks in the mirror before walking out, and even asks someone to check his appearance. A moment of humility while someone else adjusts an unbalanced chasuble surpasses causing an hour's visual distraction to the faithful.

Liturgical processions call for a dignified pace. Especially when wearing vestments, a priest's measured pace makes a difference. He dresses differently at Mass than he does for any other activity. Mass begins with a solemn processing, not with expedient dashing. Some priests would begin the liturgy in a more intentional way if they just walked more slowly.

No rubrics govern how to stand when praying or reading. Still, a good spiritual principle is to hold one's body erect, straightening the spine and balancing one's weight on both feet. Slouching suggests unimportance. Attention to the body can make a priest feel as ready as a soldier, especially when addressing God.

No rubrics tell the priest how to hold his hands when he is standing but not praying. Some priests close their hands, crossing their thumbs, their fingers pointed straight out together. Others fold their hands palm to palm, the fingers of one hand nesting between the thumb and fingers of the other. Dropping one's arms to one's sides, however, will convey an attitude of inattention. A priest should stand in a way that helps him pay attention and helps others realize he has closed his hands to every other activity besides the one he now attends.

The priest extends his hands as he greets the people or prays. The Missal used to explain how high and wide to hold hands at such time. It no longer does so. It trusts the priest's good judgment. Many priests distinguish the extension of hands when greeting the people from the extension of hands when saying a prayer. When greeting the people, some extend their hands in a forward motion; when saying a prayer some extend them to the sides in imitation of figures in ancient Christian art striking the *orans* (or "praying") position. However a priest does it, this latter extension of his hands should feel prayerful to him and look prayerful to the people. From time to time, a vested priest may use the sacristy mirror to see what people see when he extends his hands. How does it look?

The three-part dialogue that opens the eucharistic prayer has the priest adjust his arms with each phrase he says. He greets the people while "extending his hands," so the words and action fit together. He raises his hands when inviting them to lift their hearts. Then, "with hands extended," he invites them to give thanks (OM 31). In this last case, the hands are in position before he speaks the words. Many priests use three different gestures here: the first one forward, the second up, and the third out.

Bows and genuflections are signs of reverence and deserve intentionality and dignity. They draw attention to an object of devotion. It benefits a priest to think about these actions. Why offer reverence to this object at this time? What is its purpose? In its presence, what attitude befits a priest?

When sitting, a priest is not just resting. He always pays full attention. The presider's bodily posture during the Liturgy of the Word should signal to everyone the importance of the readings and the psalm. Some priests mistakenly use the first two readings to review the notes of their homily, to find a page in the Missal, to check a participation aid, to switch off a cellphone, or whisper instructions to the servers. A priest has one duty during the Liturgy of the Word: to listen. It requires full attention. The best practice is to listen without referencing a copy of the readings. The prepared presider is so familiar with them that he needs no visual aid. As the scriptures are read aloud, God is speaking the divine word in the church right now (GIRM 29).

A presider may be distracted by the way the reader dressed, approached the sanctuary, opened the book, failed to adjust the microphone, spoke in the wrong volume, avoided proper eye contact, or mispronounced words. At this moment, none of it matters. The presider can deal with those important directives sometime after Mass. In this moment God is speaking through the word. If a priest opens his ears and not his analytical field, he may hear something even in an inadequate proclamation that had not struck him before. The liturgy happens in the moment. A good *ars celebrandi* means entering the moment uncritically, humbly, while listening attentively to the Word of the Lord.

When the psalmist invites all to sing, the invitation includes the presider. Exteriorly he models participation in the responsorial, and interiorly he makes these words his own. He not only sings the words; he prays the words. They become his words. A presider is sitting, but he is totally occupied with participation in the now.

Actions

Intentionality includes doing one thing at a time. A good *ars celebrandi* keeps the presider singular in focus during each activity of the Mass. At work, nearly every priest multitasks. Mass is not the time to show off that skill. Less is more. A priest enhances his intentionality when he focuses on one thing at a time.

A good *ars celebrandi* avoids speaking while flipping pages. For example, after saying the prayer over the offerings, a priest may realize he forgot to set the ribbon for the preface. He starts flipping pages. If he senses an unexpected lull in the service, he may erroneously conclude that speech is better than silence. Hands occupied with finding the right page, a distracted presider may throw out lines to the people without really meaning them or using the appropriate gestures. "The Lord be with you," he says, but casting his eyes onto the Missal while turning its pages. "Lift up your hearts," he says, as if expecting the Missal to react. He might as well be saying to the people, "You lift them up right now because I'm busy with something else." It would probably take less than one minute to find the proper page. Silence is better than doing two things at a time and giving insufficient attention to the meaning of the words.

Setting the Missal's ribbons ahead of time remedies this scenario. It demands some time and attention, a bit of preparation before Mass begins, but is worth every moment. Considering all the options a priest has especially on weekdays in Ordinary Time, setting the ribbons can express his preparatory meditation for the liturgy of the day.

The Creed is another moment when some priests do two things at a time. For example, for the universal prayer, some priests read the introduction and conclusion from the Missal or another printed aid. They may want the server in place, holding the material before the Creed is over. Sometimes the server does not realize this. Sometimes the priest seeks to correct the server's distraction by creating a distraction himself, so as not to lose a single second between the end of the Creed and the start of the universal prayer. He cannot successfully do these two things at the same time: He cannot simultaneously signal the server and attentively confess his belief in the Holy Spirit.

Sometimes priests pay little attention to the rest of the Creed. They talk to the deacon. They look anxiously for the person who will read the petitions. They check their watch. All of this distracts them from professing their faith and sets the wrong example for the people over whom he presides.

The collection gathers the people's sacrifices offered to God with the bread and wine. The collection takes time, so many priests execute other actions that belong to the preparation of the gifts while the collection is underway. In egregious cases, the collection continues into the eucharistic prayer. Such behavior signals to the people that getting their money outweighs getting their participation at Mass. The collection represents the people's offering of sacrifice. A respectful *ars celebrandi* calls for the priest to sit and wait. He then receives the gifts of the people together with the bread and wine. This shows deference to the people who are sacrificing for the parish, and it encourages them to pay full attention to the prayers, doing one thing at a time.

As the *Sanctus* draws to a close, the priest probably has to turn pages to find the rest of the eucharistic prayer. If he does this during the final words of the *Sanctus*, he telegraphs the opinion that those words, which he sings together with the people, are not important. By concentrating on each word, all the way to the end of the *Sanctus*, and waiting to turn the pages, he successfully does one thing at a time.

Some priests or musicians elide the Lamb of God into the sign of peace. The actions are quite disparate. The careful presider waits until the community has completed the sign of peace before beginning to break the bread, an action so important that it first gave the Mass its name. Nor does a careful musician begin the Lamb of God until the presider has finished the sign of peace. The sign of peace is exchanged among participants; the Lamb of God unites their voices in prayer to Christ. The actions are best executed one at a time.

The liturgical music deserves the priest's participation and patience. As Mass begins, some priests process up the aisle and arrive at the sanctuary only to discover that the musicians intend to lead several more verses of the opening hymn. Some priests like to get on with their own part of the Mass, and they consider the music an obstacle. The musician is leading the song of the assembly, however, which includes the priest's voice. If the priest has an issue with the number of verses, he best discusses this with the musician outside of Mass. During Mass, when the music is underway, its words are the focus. The discipline of paying attention to them carries spiritual benefits, even for the priest. If he sets aside his frustrations, he calms his own spirit, practices charity, and enters the mystery of the Mass in the present together with the rest of the assembly united in song.

A presider will demonstrate his respect for the sacred vessels by the way he handles them. When passing a ciborium to a communion minister, for example, he may too casually pick up the vessel and hand it off inattentively. However, it contains the Body of Christ. How much more reverent it would be for him to lift the ciborium deliberately, hold it carefully, fully face the minister, and pass it from the center of his person to the hands waiting to receive it. Some Asian cultures practice an admirable custom: Those who carry sacred vessels from the sanctuary to the communion stations hold them slightly elevated near their heads, not low, to show the dignity of what they carry.

Overall, the presider holds responsibility for the smooth unfolding of the liturgy's various parts. Hovda explains,

> A good presider will keep [the parts] moving, accenting the important elements, playing down the less important, with a hand always on the thread of prayer and praise and purpose that runs through the whole service, making sure that transitions from one part to another are appropriately defined, clear, calm and unsurprising.[2]

Expressive Signs

Although less is more, intentionality often pairs well with an expressive use of signs. A profound bow shows deep interior respect and sends a better signal of reverence when the minister executes it fully, slowly and meaningfully. Incense expresses its purposes when the people can smell its aroma and see its smoke. The washing of hands looks more like a purification rite if the server pours a stream of water across the priest's hands and then offers him a suitable towel. An abundant use of water and chrism proclaims the pivotal meaning of baptism. The Missal declares the importance of signs:

> Since, however, the celebration of the Eucharist, like the entire Liturgy, is carried out by means of perceptible signs by which the faith is nourished, strengthened, and expressed, the greatest care is to be taken that those forms and elements proposed by the Church are chosen and arranged, which, given the circumstances of persons and places, more effectively foster active and full participation and more aptly respond to the spiritual needs of the faithful.[3]

An expressive use of signs is most appropriate when it enriches people's attention to the liturgy, not their attention to the presider. As any excess may distort the use of signs, so may minimalism.

[2] Hovda, *Strong, Loving and Wise*, p. 60.

[3] GIRM 20. See also my treatment in *Let Us Pray: A Guide to the Rubrics of Sunday Mass, Updated to Conform with the Revised English Translation of The Roman Missal* (Collegeville, MN: Liturgical Press, 2012), pp. 4–6.

4

Intentionality in Word

The presider uses his voice in a variety of ways: prayers and dialogues with the people, homilies, unscripted remarks, and private prayers. Proper attention to these develops an improved *ars celebrandi*.

Prayers and Dialogues

A priest's prayers and dialogues with the people most importantly invite his intentionality. When addressing the people, the presider introduces a conversation with them. An integrated *ars celebrandi* makes the interaction sound like genuine communication.

Presidential prayers in general

Violinist Isaac Stern used to tell his students, "Don't use music to play the violin. Use the violin to play music." In the liturgical setting one could advise a priest, "Don't use the Missal to recite a prayer; use prayer to recite the Missal."

When the presider reads a prayer, he owes it to himself, to the people, and to God to give meaning to the scripted words with his voice. Although the words are printed in the Missal, an *ars celebrandi* makes them sound as if the priest composed them and is praying them from his heart, as if they express his ideas now, not some abstract words on a page. Some priests erroneously read the collects and eucharistic prayers as if they were a task to be dispatched rather than an appeal to God.

Some priests read the presidential prayers and especially the eucharistic prayer quickly, as if the great number of words demands a more advanced tempo. For many people, the speed of the prayer obstructs their ability to pray along and makes it appear that the priest himself cannot possibly be meditating on the words that he reads so quickly. A measured pace will usually help the priest intend the meaning of each word and facilitate the prayer of the assembly.

Some priests object to the translation of the prayers in the Missal. They find the grammar convoluted and the vocabulary obscure.[1] Indeed, there are problems with many parts. Even so, the Missal now shows greater sensitivity to the content of the prayers, some of which enjoy considerable antiquity in ancestral Missals, bringing forth greater theological depth and richer allusions to the Scriptures. A priest who studies the history, purpose, and grammar of these prayers in advance will offer them more clearly.

Even with prayers he does not like, a presider benefits from getting inside them, reading them with understanding and devotion. In this way he remains faithful to the liturgy and helpful to the people. The prayers may provide spiritual formation even to a resistant priest when they realign the way he may have prayed otherwise.

The GIRM asks all worshipers to understand the genre of the words and to speak them accordingly:

> In texts that are to be pronounced in a loud and clear voice, whether by the Priest or the Deacon, or by a reader, or by everyone, the voice should correspond to the genre of the text itself, that is, depending upon whether it is a reading, a prayer, an explanatory comment, an acclamation, or a sung text; it should also be suited to the form of celebration and to the solemnity of the gathering. (80)

[1] In the interests of disclosure, I do some work for the International Commission on English in the Liturgy (ICEL) that developed the present translation.

The eucharistic prayer demands special attention. Some people mistakenly hold that this prayer belongs to the priest alone while other worshipers await their turn. But because all the faithful are baptized members of a royal priesthood, and because the full, conscious, active participation of the people is the aim to be considered above all others, the eucharistic prayer belongs to the people as well. They join in its opening dialogue, and they hand off the prayer to the priest by declaring, "It is right and just." He grasps the baton and relays, "It is truly right and just," as he begins the preface. All sing the *Sanctus*, a constitutive part of the eucharistic prayer, and then the priest vocalizes the rest on behalf of the people. The people are expected to pray along.

> Now the center and high point of the entire celebration begins, namely, the Eucharistic Prayer itself, that is, the prayer of thanksgiving and sanctification. The Priest calls upon the people to lift up their hearts towards the Lord in prayer and thanksgiving; he associates the people with himself in the Prayer that he addresses in the name of the entire community to God the Father through Jesus Christ in the Holy Spirit. Furthermore, the meaning of this Prayer is that the whole congregation of the faithful joins with Christ in confessing the great deeds of God and in the offering of Sacrifice. The Eucharistic Prayer requires that everybody listens to it with reverence and in silence. (GIRM 78)

The GIRM calls for the participation of the entire congregation. The very meaning of the eucharistic prayer asks them to join with Christ in two priestly actions: confessing God's great deeds and offering sacrifice. The GIRM calls for the priest to behave accordingly: He associates the people with himself in this prayer. It is not his private prayer to be offered in a low voice. It is to be pronounced "loud and clear" (GIRM 38), and indeed, prayerfully, meaningfully.

When priests first offered these prayers aloud in the vernacular languages, they had little training for it. Of course, they could read their own language, but now they were leading people in vernacular prayer as never before. Just three years into the new Order of Mass, the Sacred Congregation for Divine Worship addressed some concerns that were already being shared about proclaiming the eucharistic prayer. The congregation opened with a reminder that the reforms "are intended above all to facilitate intelligent, devout, active participation by the faithful in the Eucharist."[2] It continued,

> a truly living and communal celebration requires that the one presiding and the others who have some particular function to perform should give thought to the various forms of verbal communication with the congregation, namely, the readings, homily admonitions, introductions and the like.[3]
>
> In reciting prayers, especially the Eucharistic Prayer, the priest must avoid not only a dry, monotonous style of reading but an overly subjective and emotional manner of speaking and acting as well. As he presides over the function, he must be careful in reading, singing or acting to help the participants form a true community, celebrating and living the memorial of the Lord.[4]

Thus, even in 1973, only a few years into the first English translation, some priests did not realize their duty or failed to attune their voice to the words they spoke.

The Missal provides formulas for chanting the presidential prayers, and the GIRM encourages the priest to sing the eucharistic prayer as well (147). A singing presider can add solemnity to the celebration. This does not happen as frequently in the United States as in countries such as England and Vietnam. A priest who becomes comfortable with the chants will find that singing the prayers is prayerful in a different way. It decreases the amount of variation in his voice, subjecting the priest even more to the Missal's words, while still permitting him to adjust the pacing that can interpret them. Reciting prayers employs other skills such as inflection and volume to interpret the words. When singing, a careful priest draws attention not to himself, but to the meaning of the words. A priest exercising good *ars celebrandi*

[2] Sacred Congregation for Divine Worship, Circular Letter to the Presidents of the National Conferences of Bishops on Eucharistic Prayers, *Eucharistiæ Participationem* (April 27, 1973), https://www.evangelizationstation.com/htm_html/Church%20Documents/Documents%20on%20Mass%20&%20Eucharist/circular_letter_to_the_president.htm, 1.

[3] GIRM 18.

[4] Circular Letter to the Presidents, 17.

always wants to associate the people with himself while he prays (GIRM 78).

All of this presumes that the priest is a man familiar with prayer. When he correctly says the few words, "Let us pray," the people will immediately feel that he knows what he's talking about. He is familiar with the world of prayer, and he is now offering them a guided tour. The presider invites people into the quiet space he has created within himself, the space where he once found his own vocation, the space where he still encounters God quite deeply, the center from which a priest draws spiritual breath. When he prays out loud in public, the words are all to come from that sacred, interior space.

Understanding the structure of the eucharistic prayer and the collects of the Roman Missal may help the priest enter into them more meaningfully.

The eucharistic prayer

The GIRM outlines the skeleton of a eucharistic prayer (79). It omits a few parts that have been added below in brackets for the sake of clarity.

[Dialogue]. The prayer opens with a dialogue between the priest and the people. An inviting tone in his words will best match the message and purpose of the gestures.

Thanksgiving. In GIRM 79 this refers to the preface. Every preface gives thanks to God for something. No preface asks God to do anything. The entire prayer is "eucharistic," which means "of thanksgiving." The preface sets the tone for everything that follows.

Acclamation. GIRM 79 uses this word to refer to the *Sanctus*. The people, the ministers and the entire heavenly host make this acclamation together.

[Thanksgiving.] Although GIRM 79 does not mention it, the spirit of thanksgiving continues immediately after the *Sanctus*. Some of the prayers deliver a rather long, developed section, notably Eucharistic Prayer IV. Others, like Prayer II, keep it brief. Regardless, the *Sanctus* ends, and the thanksgiving returns before the prayer enters its next critical juncture.

Epiclesis. The priest asks the Father to send the Holy Spirit to change the bread and wine into the Body and Blood of Christ. A priest does not singlehandedly effect this change; he asks for the Holy Spirit to do that. The Eastern Rites of the church regard this as the most sacred moment of the prayer. If a Western mind asks an Eastern colleague, "When is the moment of consecration?" the response may come reluctantly because of the reverence paid the entire eucharistic prayer in the East, but it will probably indicate the epiclesis. However, the Eastern prayers have the epiclesis after the account of the Last Supper. That account, which the GIRM calls the institution narrative, is part of the thanksgiving, one reason for which the priest gives thanks to God. Even in the Roman Missal, the institution narrative falls into this category of thanksgiving. The Missal, however, has the epiclesis in this forward position, where it sets the complete thanksgiving on pause. The Roman Canon has no explicit epiclesis. It is implied with the words "make them spiritual," when the priest extends his hands over the offerings as for the epiclesis in the other prayers. Probably because the Roman Canon had no explicit epiclesis, its moment of consecration defaulted to the repetition of the words of Christ, "This is my Body." "This is my Blood."

Institution narrative and consecration. The GIRM joins these two concepts. In the narration of the Last Supper, the institution of the Eucharist, the church believes that the bread and wine are consecrated into the Body and Blood of Christ. Many priests and lay people will fail to answer this question correctly: When the priest says, "Take this all of you and eat of it," to whom is he speaking? Many Catholics assume that the priest is speaking to the people, inviting them to take and eat. However, he is not speaking to them. He is speaking to the Father: "giving you [Father] thanks, . . . [and] saying, 'take this all of you [disciples].' " The priest quotes what Jesus said to the disciples, but he is recounting the narrative of the institution of the Eucharist in his prayer of thanksgiving to the Father. He is not addressing the people. The entire eucharistic prayer is a seamless address to the Father.

[Memorial acclamation.] The priest proclaims—not really to the people, not really to God—but as if in wonder to the air, "The mystery of faith." The people respond with an acclamation. Even here, the

priest is not directly addressing the people. He's launching a cue for them to acclaim Christ. They address Christ in words such as, "We proclaim your death, O Lord," because Christ is truly present under the forms of bread and wine on the altar. This is the only moment in the entire eucharistic prayer when anyone addresses the Second Person of the Trinity. The acclamation belongs to the people. The priest is not supposed to respond with them. He gives the cue. They acclaim Christ. He remains silent until they conclude. Then he returns to his prayer, staying spiritually centered the entire time on his address to the Father. In practice, the priest often leads the people's acclamation, especially if it is spoken. But the people may agree to a single acclamation, at least for a period of weeks or months. Or someone could begin or post the acclamation for the day. The priest will probably feel more engaged in his duties if he does not shift focus and address Christ in the middle of his prayer to the Father.

Anamnesis. The prayer remembers the first coming of Christ, his death and resurrection, and it looks for him to return. The priest is covering similar material that the people just sang. Unlike the people, however, he is addressing the Father.

Oblation. Wrapped inside the anamnesis, inseparable from it, is the oblation or offering. To speak of the sacrifice of the Mass is to allude to this moment. Every prayer includes this phrase at this point: "We offer you." This main verb enfolds two elements, the anamnesis and the oblation: "as we remember, we offer." When reciting the eucharistic prayer, the presider becomes more mindful if he slows down at the word "sacrifice", ensuring all the priestly people gathered of his attention to their sacrificial responsibility as well.

Intercessions. The eucharistic prayer saves other requests for the end: the needs of the church, the pope, the bishop, the living, and the dead. It's as if the priest is thinking, "Now that we've got God's attention, there are a few more things we'd like to request."

Concluding dialogue. The prayer concludes through, with, and in Christ in the unity of the Holy Spirit. All answer "Amen." This is another dialogue. The priest does not sing the amen here any more than he says it after the collect. The people's "Amen" affirms all that the priest has said.

The collect

A typical collect has an identifiable structure, though the GIRM does not explain it. Not every collect follows the same structure but knowing its parts can help the priest and the people interpret its meaning.[5]

Invocation. The priest addresses God by some title, such as Father, Lord, God, or any of the above with an adjective, such as Holy Father or Almighty God.

Amplification. The priest declares something that God has done; for example, "who created the world in all its wonder," or "who forgive your people even when we stray." In many collects, this amplification relates to other parts of the prayer. The community is praising God for something in the past that pertains to the request that this prayer makes in present.

Petition. This is the heart of the collect. The reason the assembly wants God's attention at all is to ask for something. "Send us the rain we need." "Forgive the sins of your people." "Heal the sick among us." Everything up to this point has been smoothing the way to this request. Not all collects follow this procedure. Some immediately blurt out the request without any hemming or hawing.

Motive. The collect may also tell God what prompts this petition. "Our crops are failing." "Our conscience is bothering us." "This community feels lost." The motive explains the reason for the appeal. Good fundraising techniques inform the donor about the need. The same happens here.

Purpose. This expresses what will result if God favorably answers the prayer. "Your people will be fed." "All nations will come to know your mercy." "We can praise you evermore." The collect often shows that God will also benefit by granting the petition.

Conclusion. The prayer concludes with a recognizable formula: "Through our Lord Jesus Christ your Son," and so on. The Missal

[5] I rely on the work of Renato de Zan, Daniel McCarthy, and James Leachman. See, for example, Daniel P. McCarthy, James G. Leachman, *Listen to the Word: Commentaries on Selected Opening Prayers of Sundays and Feasts with Sample Homilies* (London: The Tablet, 2009).

gives only a couple of variations on this, making it easier for all to respond "Amen."

Awareness of these components helps analyze a collect. For example, on the Third Sunday of Lent, the collect comes from the seventh-century Gelasian Sacramentary on Saturday of the Fourth Week of Lent. It replaces one from the preconciliar Roman Missal, which asked God to extend his right hand to defend the humble who offer these prayers. Apparently, the compilers of the post–Vatican II Missal thought that the prayer from the Gelasian was richer. One can easily discern the component parts of this expressive collect.

> O God [*invocation*], author of every mercy and of all goodness
> [*amplification*],
> who in fasting, prayer and almsgiving
> have shown us a remedy for sin [*more amplification*],
> look graciously on this confession of our lowliness [*petition*],
> that we, who are bowed down by our conscience [*motive*],
> may always be lifted up by your mercy [*purpose*].
> Through our Lord Jesus Christ [*conclusion*]. . . .

When offering this prayer, a sincere presider will get in touch with his own conscience. How is it bothering him? What has he done that needs forgiveness? If the people are wondering the same thing about themselves, this prayer truly reflects the contrition of all. The petition for this eloquent prayer sets a pretty low bar: It asks God to look—nothing more, just to look on this confession of sin. God is generous, but the priest approaches humbly, not arrogantly, not presumptuously, as he would any donor in the parish. Deference prompts a favorable response to needs.

On the Third Sunday of Advent, the collect comes from the Rotulus of Ravenna. The Rotulus, or "little rolled-up volume," is a collection of prayers from the fifth or sixth century, some of the oldest collects known. Gathered onto vellum in eighth-century Ravenna, the written prayers span nearly four yards. Somebody lost it, so the pre–Vatican II Missal knew nothing about it. It was rediscovered in the nineteenth century, and the post–Vatican II Missal included some of its treasured prayers. This one is probably the oldest documented Advent prayer in the history of Christianity:

> O God [*invocation*], who see [*amplification*] how your people
> faithfully await the feast of the Lord's Nativity [*motive*],
> enable us, we pray,
> to attain the joys of so great a salvation [*petition*]
> and to celebrate them always
> with solemn worship and glad rejoicing [*another petition*].
> Through our Lord Jesus Christ [*conclusion*]. . . .

This collect lacks an expressed purpose, but God would certainly welcome the reputation of causing solemn worship and glad rejoicing.

One final example comes from the Third Sunday of Easter. This collect was created for the post–Vatican II Missal. The compilers stitched together elements from two different prayers, one from Easter in the Gelasian Sacramentary and another from a Mass for the Dead in the Verona Sacramentary, a century earlier. The result appears again as an optional collect for the extended Vigil on Pentecost. The preconciliar collect for the Third Sunday of Easter, because of its more generic theme, moved to the Fourteenth Sunday in Ordinary Time. For Easter Time, the Missal now presents a series of collects that celebrate the joy of the season. This is but one example.

> May your people exult for ever [*petition*], O God [*invocation*],
> in renewed youthfulness of spirit,
> so that, rejoicing now in the restored glory of our adoption [*motive*],
> we may look forward in confident hope
> to the rejoicing of the day of resurrection [*purpose*].
> Through our Lord Jesus Christ [*conclusion*]. . . .

This prayer leads with its request and omits any amplification for God. Filled with the exuberance of Easter, it turns to God like a happy kid to provident parents, "I wish this birthday would last forever!" All it requests is eternal exultation.

Thinking back on the GIRM's admonishments that priests should attune their voice to the genre of the prayer, a careful presider contrasts the penitential tone of the collect on the Third Sunday of Lent with the exultant tone on the Third Sunday of Easter. A priest with a good *ars celebrandi* will detect and express the difference. In both cases, he will not simply be reading the words. He will pray them with intentionality.

Dialogues

The presider engages the participation of the people in a special way through the dialogues. In the past, the priest conducted the dialogues principally with the altar servers. One hallmark of the twentieth century liturgical renewal brought the congregation into the dialogues in real time. Calling them "responses," the Constitution on the Sacred Liturgy named them as one example of the active participation of the people (SC 30).

Those responses come alive especially when they form the back end of a true dialogue in which the person who initiated the greeting awaits a reply. When one person says "Good morning" to another, the originator of the dialogue does not then say "Good morning" back to himself. He or she expects the other person to return the greeting. The same takes place at Mass. The people are expected to make a wide range of responses within the dialogues, far more complex than a mere "Good morning." They have learned these and can respond well—if given the chance.

However, some priests—and deacons—make the response that the people are supposed to shoulder for themselves. These clergy probably think that they are being helpful. But such behavior keeps people from learning these responses and makes them feel unwelcome to say them. For example, the minister is to say, "The Gospel of the Lord," but not the response. That is for the people to do. If they do not respond well this week, they will learn in the weeks to come, but not if the one who proclaims the gospel speaks both parts of the dialogue.

Some dialogues are hidden in plain sight. When the priest begins Mass, he says the sign of the cross, but he does not add "Amen." That is for the people to say. After the Lord's Prayer the priest prays the embolism. It concludes with a dialogue. The people—not the priest—say, "For the kingdom, the power and the glory are yours now and for ever." As with the memorial acclamation and the eucharistic prayer's concluding amen, the careful presider does not respond to his own invitation.

In the distribution of communion the dialogue is intense and personal. One by one the minister and communicant exchange their belief in the Body and Blood of Christ. The minister has only a moment to convey this and to anticipate the communicant's response.

Sometimes the minister appears distracted by something else in the room or by someone else in the line. But in the moment of distributing communion, intentionality demands full concentration on the dialogue with each and every communicant. The Order of Mass does not invite any variation in the formula for distributing communion, not even the addition of the communicant's name. By using the identical formula for each communicant, the minister invites an ever-deepening meditation on the Body and Blood of Christ.

When a presider pays attention to such refinements, he deepens his appreciation of the role of the people. His role is to associate the people with himself in this prayer and to enliven their ability to participate.

Homilies

The homily is one of the most important events of a priest's week. The faithful listen attentively in hopes of improving their spiritual lives, moral decision-making, catechesis, and motivation to evangelize. They will come to know their priest better through his preaching. They'll learn his values and priorities, his ability to think and communicate clearly, his commitment to the gospel, and his love for the community. Even if a priest divulges little of his personal life, people will learn about him every time he preaches.

As private prayer prepares a priest to lead public prayer, so private prayer helps him preach. The time he spends with the Scriptures will form his own encounter with God, strengthening him to preach the Good News. Through this time of private prayer, a preacher outlines his homily. People appreciate a thoughtful presentation, well-organized and inspiring, attentive to detail.

Resources

Resources for good preaching abound. Several in particular deserve mention.

Evangelii Gaudium. Pope Francis wrote this apostolic exhortation in 2013, the first year of his pontificate, to encourage evangelization and to enliven the joy the gospel brings believers. He devoted the entire third chapter, the middle of the exhortation, to "The Proclamation of the Gospel." Preachers will find inspiration and practical advice for homily preparation.[6]

For example, Pope Francis speaks about spending time with the word in prayer, with "humble and awe-filled veneration . . . and a holy fear lest we distort it" (146). Citing Pope John Paul II in *Pastores Dabo Vobis* (26), Pope Francis says that a priest "needs to approach the word with a docile and prayerful heart so that it may deeply penetrate his thoughts and feelings" (149). A priest should listen to his people to discover what they need to hear; he "has to contemplate the word, but he also has to contemplate his people" (154). Pope Francis says that a good homily is positive (159). After all, it preaches the Good News. He criticizes preachers who think that they know what needs to be said, but who do not know how to say it. "They complain when people do not listen to or appreciate them, but perhaps they have never taken the trouble to find the proper way of presenting their message" (156).

Homiletic Directory. Two years after Pope Francis's exhortation, the Vatican's Congregation for Divine Worship and the Discipline of the Sacraments (CDWDS) issued a homiletic directory.[7] Its first half gives guidelines for preaching, and the entire second half shares reflections on each Sunday gospel passage of the liturgical year. The heading is *ars predicandi*, the art of preaching. Cynics who think that nothing good comes out of Roman congregations will be surprised at the pastoral, helpful tone of this directory.

The Homiletic Directory opens with four themes of perennial importance: the Word of God in the liturgy, biblical interpretation, the biblical understanding that shapes a priest's homily and his own spiritual life, and the needs of those to whom the preaching is directed (2). It notes that prayer is essential: The homily "should be composed

[6] Apostolic Exhortation *Evangelii Gaudium* of the Holy Father Francis to the Bishops, Clergy, Consecrated Persons and the Lay Faithful on the Proclamation of the Gospel in Today's World (November 24, 2013), http://www.vatican.va/content/francesco/en/apost_exhortations/documents/papa-francesco_esortazione-ap_20131124_evangelii-gaudium.html.

[7] Congregation for Divine Worship and the Discipline of the Sacraments, Homiletic Directory (Vatican City: Libreria Editrice Vaticana, 2015), https://www.vatican.va/roman_curia/congregations/ccdds/documents/rc_con_ccdds_doc_20140629_direttorio-omiletico_en.html.

in a context of prayer" (26). The homily distributes God's word to the people, anticipating the distributing of communion later in the Mass (26). The directory recommends prayer with *lectio divina*, as described by Pope Benedict XVI (27).

Preaching the Mystery of Faith: The Sunday Homily. Just before both of these Vatican publications, the USCCB had issued its own recommendations for the Sunday homily in 2012.[8] The bishops call for "urgency and freshness" in preaching (10). The homilist is to make the reality of his faith "visible and radiant" (12). A homily preaches "the dying and rising of Jesus Christ" (15) and "ought to inspire a sense of mission" (18). A homily is "an invaluable opportunity to advance the Church's catechetical ministry" (21). On days such as Christmas and Easter when occasional worshipers frequent a church, "This is obviously not the time to chide such Catholics for their absence" (25).

These three extraordinary documents show the highest level of church authority encouraging homilists to preach better and offering guidelines to help. Reading these statements will not automatically improve one's preaching, any more than reading a book on playing the piano will automatically impart that skill. But these resources will help each preacher recommit to the fundamental purpose of the homily and to approach it with joyful faith, a healthy fear of God's word, and love for the people.

Composition

Writing out the complete homily can help a preacher develop his thought, control the message, and gain confidence. He can create images and expressions without fear of forgetting them in the moment. He can repeat certain words or phrases at key junctures to unify the homily. He can also manage the word count. Limiting a homily to six hundred words, for example, can teach precision in thought. A consistent length helps people listen.

[8] *Preaching the Mystery of Faith: The Sunday Homily* (Washington, DC: United States Conference of Catholic Bishops, 2012), http://www.usccb.org/beliefs-and-teachings/vocations/priesthood/priestly-life-and-ministry/upload/usccb-preaching-document.pdf.

The homily resembles an essay. The opening words set the direction toward the closing words. Some priests use the opening to greet groups, make announcements, or comment on the Mass so far. They imply that they haven't yet been able to share themselves with the people, and that this is their moment. They treat the opening of the homily like an after-dinner speech. The first few words, however—in some cases the very first word—best launch the theme of the words to follow. The complete homily is to integrate with the liturgy of the day.

Some priests preach effectively without text or notes, but they have done their homework ahead of time and they rise to the moment. Other preachers without notes cannot clearly develop a thought on the fly and struggle to bring a talk to a conclusion.

A priest who preaches without a text may benefit from listening to a recording of his homily, or better yet, reading a complete transcription of what he actually said. The length of his sentences and his inaccurate use of grammar may surprise him. He may also find that he did not quite phrase something the way he wanted, or that he communicated something he does not believe at all.

Posting homilies online will extend their reach. Some homilists say that they do not preach well enough to be live-streamed or posted. If a homily is not good enough for the internet, however, then it is not good enough for the congregation. The people deserve the best. Someone may be recording anyway. Especially at funerals and weddings, the homily will likely be preserved for generations to come. If a serious preacher thinks his homily is not that good, he goes back to work to revise it.

The length of the homily is often the source of greatest criticism. However, this criticism may represent something else: flow. If the direction of thought is too hard to follow, the homily seems longer than it really is. People yearn for an ending because they are lost in the forest, and they cannot see the way out.

The contours of the liturgy similarly dictate the length of the homily. The Mass is not a frame for one's preaching. Preaching serves the Liturgy of the Word, and the highlight of presiding is the eucharistic prayer, not the homily. Some priests preach so long that they rush the rest of the Mass, circumventing the impatience of the people by choosing Eucharistic Prayer II. Such presiders may be guilty of either poor preparation or hubris.

In general, priests care about the church, their ministry, and their people. They take homilies seriously. They know that people depend on them. They want to do a good job, so they aim for their best. Not every preacher has the same gifts. All priests are good at something. Not all preach well. Every preacher can improve with proper attention to the art.

Unscripted Remarks

The presider has freedom to use his own words at several parts of the Mass. The GIRM delineates these:

> an introduction to the Mass of the day (after the initial Greeting and before the Penitential Act), to the Liturgy of the Word (before the readings), and to the Eucharistic Prayer (before the Preface), though never during the Eucharistic Prayer itself; he may also make concluding comments regarding the entire sacred action before the Dismissal. (31)

Whenever the liturgy turns a priest loose like this, it asks him to use only a few words. Few do.

Of these four options, priests commonly exercise only the first. Many priests like to give an introduction to the Mass. But very few introduce the readings, announce reasons for giving thanks before the preface, or make comments about the Mass before the dismissal.

Regarding the first, this introduction comes after the sign of the cross and the greeting, and before the penitential act. Some presiders erroneously take the mic after the opening hymn and say, "Good morning, everyone! It's nice to see you all today!" They may then give an overview of the day, the events, the readings, and the homily, *before* making the sign of the cross. The Mass is not built that way. After the opening hymn, the sign of the cross comes first. Everything is placed under the cross, including the introductory comments. The greeting ("The Lord be with you" or one of the other options) is just that. It is the way that the priest greets the people. If he still feels the need to say "Good morning," then he may not be saying the greeting with the right intention. It replaces "Good morning." The secular greeting has no place here because the liturgical greeting conveys its message plus much more. It wishes not just a good morning, but the presence of the Lord.

Even at the two largest celebrations of the year, an intentional presider says, "Merry Christmas!" or "Happy Easter!" only after the sign of the cross and the liturgical greeting of the Mass. The extra greeting may then further unify the people and express the joy of the day's gathering.

The second option in GIRM 31 is an introduction to the readings. Very few priests do this. It can sound pedantic, especially if the homily explores the same readings. An introduction to the day's Scriptures is permitted, but not recommended if it is repetitious or dense.

As a third option, before the preface dialogue, the priest may offer reasons for giving thanks. Not many priests exercise this option. A careful presider may at least pause a moment between the prayer over the offerings and the eucharistic prayer. This helps distinguish their purpose and lets him draw a deep breath before beginning a project that demands full attention. Few priests fill that space with reasons for thanksgiving, possibly because it seems to restrain the mood rather than enhance it.

The fourth option is not the announcements, but to summarize some point from the Mass before the dismissal. In practice, it functions as the last announcement. The priest could recall a line from the gospel of the day before giving the blessing. For example, he could say, "Jesus says, 'Love God and love your neighbor.' The Lord be with you." Then he may proceed with the blessing, and Mass concludes with the dismissal. It can flow nicely, but not many presiders do it.

GIRM 31 mentions four places where the priest has freedom to speak in his own words. However, he has other opportunities that deserve thoughtful preparation.

The penitential act. The introduction to the penitential act may be abbreviated or expanded. The brief introduction envisioned in GIRM 31 may lean its final words into the penitential act. A presider who scripts out an introduction specific to each week can more easily avoid repeating generic thoughts week after week. When using the third form of the penitential act, the presider may compose his own invocations to Christ, even if someone else reads them. Appendix VI of the Missal contains helpful examples. The invocations are acclamations to Christ who is merciful, not appeals to Christ to show mercy. Although a well-crafted introduction can help the Sunday assembly transition from the outside world into interior reflection, a weekday assembly may not require much persuasion. A simple introduction may suffice, such as "Let us acknowledge our sins." Those words are better than "Let us call to mind our sins," a mental activity that could itself become an occasion of sin.

The universal prayer. The presider may compose his own introduction and conclusion to the universal prayer (the prayer over the people). Writing these out in advance assures a thoughtful, varied, and pertinent presentation. Priests who improvise their introductions and conclusions are probably not as creative as they think. Many presiders have settled on one or two formulas that they keep repeating. Some priests believe that they could write better prayers than the collects of the Missal. They have an opportunity every day to do just that as they conclude the universal prayer. Yet many do not take the time to compose. A thoughtful introduction and closing prayer may draw inspiration from the readings of the day or the community's social or seasonal climate. They help the priest become more intentional as he begins and concludes this prayer of the people.

The Lord's Prayer. The priest may vary the introduction to the Lord's Prayer.[9] A short introduction usually works because people know what to do, and less is more. It could shift for a season; for example, during Advent, "Let us pray for the coming of God's kingdom as

[9] See my book *In These or Similar Words: Praying and Crafting the Language of the Liturgy* (Franklin Park, IL: World Library Publications, 2014; now distributed through GIA Publications) pp. 21, 36–37, referring to Sacred Congregation for Divine Worship, "*Eucharistiae Participationem*, Circular Letter to the Presidents of the National Conferences of Bishops on Eucharistic Prayers, April 27, 1973," 14, which says, "importance is to be given to those admonitions prescribed in the Order of the Mass for certain rites, which are to be introduced either before the penitential act or before the Lord's Prayer. Naturally, these admonitions need not be given word for word as set out in the Missal; it may well be advisable, at least in certain instances, to adapt them somewhat to the actual circumstances of the particular gathering" (https://www.evangelizationstation.com/htm_html/Church%20Documents/Documents%20on%20Mass%20&%20Eucharist/circular_letter_to_the_president.htm).

Jesus taught us;" or during Lent, "Let us pray for the forgiveness of our sins as Jesus taught us." If the introduction is consistent in length and tone, people will know when to begin.

As Hovda wrote, "It is easy to fall into the trap of thinking that preparation and spontaneity are contradictory, or mutually exclusive."[10] A priest will probably enhance his *ars celebrandi* if he writes out the introduction to the Mass and penitential act, the introduction and conclusion to the universal prayer, and the announcements. It helps him stay focused and manage the number of spoken words.

Private Prayers

At certain points of the Mass the priest offers a prayer in private. Some priests find these at variance with the full, conscious, active participation of the people and recite them aloud. However, that is not their function. They are not dialogues; the people do not respond with an amen. Devotionally, theologically, and spiritually they remind the priest about the meaning of his actions and his preferred demeanor. They come at critical moments in the Mass. Like any other prayer, they come alive if the priest offers them intentionally.

These prayers are all that remain of a larger number in force at different times of liturgical history. They predate the era of full, conscious, active participation, and they survived it. They have a different purpose: stirring the heart of the priest who is developing the *ars* to his *celebrandi*.

The first comes before the gospel if there is no deacon. Bowing before the altar, the priest prays quietly before he greets the people at the ambo. The gospel he is about to proclaim is holy, so he asks God to cleanse his own heart and lips to proclaim it worthily. Every priest has clutched emotions and uttered words contrary to the gospel. By asking forgiveness, he prepares himself to let the words of Christ pass through his own lips.

Upon concluding the proclamation, if there is no deacon, the priest who read the gospel kisses the book and says quietly, "Through the words of the Gospel may our sins be wiped away." This humble

[10] Hovda, *Strong, Loving and Wise*, pp. 38–39.

prayer again acknowledges the priest's sinful state and his belief in the power of the proclaimed gospel. Forgiveness comes from God's word.

When adding water to the wine, the priest in the absence of a deacon prays that all may share in the divinity of Christ. This prayer comes from the same source as the collect for Christmas Mass during the day, probably composed by Pope Leo the Great. This amazing prayer contrasts mightily with the penitential tone of the prayers that bracket the gospel. This one remembers how Christ humbled himself to share humanity and—as it looks forward to communion through his Precious Blood—brazenly prays that humans may share in his divinity.

After setting the chalice on the corporal, the priest bows low and offers a prayer drawn from the Book of Daniel's account of the three young men in the fiery furnace. Both the priest and the priestly people gathered at the altar are offering the sacrifice of their lives and service to God. Before the priest begins the eucharistic prayer that includes the words of sacrifice, he prays that the sacrifices that this community offers today will be pleasing to God.

Then, as he washes his hands, he quotes Psalm 51, asking God to cleanse him of sin. As with the quiet prayers that accompany the gospel, this one recognizes that the minister is about to speak some of the most sacred words of the Mass. He prays for forgiveness before opening his mouth.

Later, after breaking the bread, the priest places a small piece in the chalice and prays that the mingling of the Body and Blood of Christ may bring eternal life to those who receive it. As with the prayer when water is added to wine, this one makes a bold request: eternal life. Incidentally, both these prayers imply communion with the Blood of Christ, strengthening the importance of sharing the chalice with the priestly people.

Before receiving communion the priest says one of two alternative prayers. The first asks God to free the priest from his sins and from every evil, keeping him faithful to the commandments. The second prays that receiving communion will not condemn him but protect and heal him in mind and body. Like the prayers before the gospel and the eucharistic prayer, these remind the priest that he is a sinner who needs pardon before he performs sacred functions.

Preparation for communion continues. In the moments before receiving the host and drinking from the chalice, the priest prays once more, this time that the Body and Blood of Christ may keep him safe for eternal life. This catches the eschatological themes of the prayers at adding water to the wine and at the commingling. As he opens his mouth to receive communion, asking forgiveness is behind him; now he looks forward to eternal life.

These themes blend when the priest purifies the vessels. The prayer that he says comes from the Verona Sacramentary, making it around 1500 years old. "What has passed our lips as food, O Lord, may we possess in purity of heart, that what has been given to us in time may be our healing for eternity" (OM 137). It intertwines the alternating themes of the other private prayers: forgiveness and eschatology.

All of these prayers are said "quietly" according to the Order of Mass. There is another part, however, where the priest speaks not "quietly" but either "in a low voice" or "aloud." This happens during the preparation of the gifts with the two prayers that begin, "Blessed are you, Lord God of all creation." He may speak aloud only if the Offertory Chant is not sung.

The preparation of the gifts was one of the last sections of the Order of Mass to be revised. The group working on the revision wanted to include the people's voice in this part of the Mass, where it had never been before.[11] The members tried several options and finally settled on this one. Their intent was to have the people either partake in the dialogue or to sing a song, bringing their voice into the preparation of the gifts. However, the final wording in the Order of Mass did not come out that way. When there is no song, the priest "may speak these words aloud" (OM 23), inviting the people's response. This gave the priest the option not to speak these words aloud even when there is no music. It would better honor the intent of the Order of Mass, however, if the priest ensured that the people used their voice in some way for the preparation of the gifts.

The phrase "in a low voice" is also used for the blessing dialogue between the priest and deacon before the deacon proclaims the gospel. This conversation takes place between the two of them, so it

[11] See my book *At the Supper of the Lamb: A Pastoral and Theological Commentary on the Mass* (Chicago: Liturgy Training Publications, 2011), pp. 52–53.

is done neither "quietly" nor "aloud." Similarly, if there is a song at the preparation of the gifts, the priest says these prayers not quietly but "in a low voice." It isn't clear why, but perhaps the deacon is to make the response since the people's voices are occupied.

In brief, these private prayers remind the priest that he remains in God's presence throughout the Mass. No other minister prays as much as the priest does publicly or privately. Prayer is the strength of the priest. It rests in his heart especially at critical junctures in the celebration of the Mass.[12]

Developing intentionality to act and to word applies to everyone at Mass, but especially the presider. As Michael Begolly points out, "By asking '*What* am I doing, and *why* am I doing what I do?" the presider can examine if both word and gesture reflect what the church intends."[13]

[12] I have treated this at greater length in *The Pastor at Prayer* (Omaha: The Institute for Priestly Formation IPF Publications, 2016).

[13] Michael J. Begolly, *Leading the Assembly in Prayer: A Practical Guide for Lay and Ordained Presiders*, rev. ed. (San Jose: Resource Publications, 2008), p. 47.

5

Interactions

The participation of the people fosters interactions among the various participants at the Mass. The Holy Spirit distributes gifts generously among the people. When each person fulfills a given ministry, the liturgy expresses itself more richly. Part of a priest's *ars celebrandi* is letting other ministers enact their responsibilities, and to provide helpful yet unobtrusive leadership as these transpire. This section examines the variety of ministers, the giving of cues, the engagement of the faithful, the importance of silence, and the question of unwelcome disturbances that create interactions when none was intended to take place.

Other Ministers

The Second Vatican Council encouraged people to exercise the diversity of their gifts. "All taking part in liturgical celebrations, whether ministers or members of the congregation, should do all that pertains to them, and no more, taking into account the rite and the liturgical norms" (SC 28). The priest, then, does well to exercise only the parts that pertain directly to him, and to encourage others to perform the other duties. Those ministers are to exercise their "genuine liturgical ministry" with their own *ars celebrandi*, "the sincere piety and decorum which is appropriate to so exalted a ministry" (SC 29).

Sacristans. Blessed is the priest who has a good sacristan. Sacristans become familiar with the requirements for the celebration of Mass, and they also learn the idiosyncrasies of each priest. Those with a knowledge of liturgy and a spirit of service provide invaluable assistance. They free the priest from some of the particulars before Mass begins. If the sacristan has not arrived because of a change in work schedule, a miscommunication of substitutes, or the tardiness of a city bus, a presider scrambles in the last moments before Mass to think through and execute what a sacristan does so well. Even at daily Mass, a sacristan can free the priest to concentrate on what he needs to do, centering his spirit properly for the celebration of the Eucharist.

Deacons. Not every priest has a deacon at his side for the Mass. Not every priest wants a deacon at his side for Mass. But the Mass was constructed with a deacon in mind. The different parts unfold more fittingly when a deacon is there to help. The priest's mantra is "Let us pray": He offers presidential prayers, the eucharistic prayer, and multiple silent prayers. The deacon's implied mantra is "Let us act": He exhorts people to offer a sign of peace, instructs them when to kneel and when to stand, and commands them to go forth. The deacon proclaims the gospel, and because of his other duties, he moves people into action by his proclamation of the sacred text. The gospel evangelizes people, brings them the words of Christ, and motivates them to behave according to its demands. A good deacon will free the priest to stay focused on his primary duty during the Mass: prayer.

Servers. The ministry of servers may involve people of all ages. By the very title of their ministry, they serve what needs to be done. Most of the tasks are simple enough for a child to do, though a wag may wonder why custom assigns children the responsibility of washing someone's hands. Training servers includes teaching them what to do before and after Mass, not just during it. Good servers do not ask unnecessary questions of the priest during the service. When they execute their responsibilities faithfully, the priest concentrates better on his particular duties.

Readers. The person responsible for proclaiming the readings is the reader, not the priest. The priest's role is to listen to the readings. By his bearing and attention, he models for everyone else what they should do; he presides by listening. The GIRM assigns the readings to an instituted lector (99), though, in his absence, other lay people proclaim the readings (101). "The lector has his own proper function . . . which he himself must carry out." (99). The GIRM never imagines that a priest is proclaiming the first readings. Even at daily Mass, this ministry belongs to a lay person.

Psalmist. The responsorial psalm is considered one of the readings of Sacred Scripture, so it too is handled by someone other than the priest. The GIRM envisions this as a separate role from the cantor of the Mass, though often it is the same person (61).

Cantor. The song leader animates the singing of the assembly. Even at daily Mass, someone besides the priest best leads the singing. Many daily Masses have no music, of course, but even a small congregation can probably handle sung dialogues and verses of well-known hymns.

Musicians. The organist and those who play other instruments contribute their considerable gifts to the community's worship. Some priests also play an instrument, but when they are presiding, they have a different role. Each person focuses on his or her own role.

Ministers of art and environment. Some priests have knowledgeable or strong opinions about decorating the church. They may assist the crew devoted to the task. People with a gift for color and spatial relationships perform a much-appreciated duty to improve the appearance of a church and help direct the prayers of the people.

Gift bearers. The gifts that belong in the procession are bread, wine, and offerings for the church or the poor. Though not required, water may be included in the procession. Other items do not belong in the procession: purificators, the corporal, extra chalices, and the finger bowl, for example. They are set at the side table before Mass. A procession of the gifts can often be managed even at a daily Mass. It involves some of the people, even those too reticent to take on a more primary role like the reader. Some priests begin Mass with the host on a paten on top of the chalice, as was formerly prescribed. The postconciliar liturgy, however, envisions that the bread and wine come to the altar at the procession of the gifts. That host, too, is part of the gift of the people of God; whenever possible, one of them best carries the priest's host together with the other gifts.

Communion ministers. Extraordinary ministers of holy communion especially help share the Blood of Christ with the faithful. Without them, there may be insufficient ministers to help the priestly people participate in the fullness of communion, especially by drinking from the chalice.

> Holy Communion has a fuller form as a sign when it takes place under both kinds. For in this form the sign of the Eucharistic banquet is more clearly evident and clearer expression is given to the divine will by which the new and eternal Covenant is ratified in the Blood of the Lord, as also the connection between the Eucharistic banquet and the eschatological banquet in the Kingdom of the Father. (GIRM 281)

This passage explains the benefits of receiving communion under both kinds. The consecrated wine more clearly indicates that the Eucharist is a banquet, both the one enjoyed on earth and the one anticipated in heaven. Moses sealed the eternal covenant with God by sprinkling the blood of a bull on the altar and upon the people (Exod 24:6-8). The new covenant is sealed with the blood of Christ, not sprinkled, but consumed by the people. These resonances of celebration, covenant, and promise reverberate when the priestly people at Mass complete their own sacrifice by participating in both the Body and the Blood of the Lord. A good *ars celebrandi* makes the cup available to the people and provides sufficient ministers for its distribution.

Ushers. In some parishes the ushers form a tightly bound community of men who collect the money and store it for safekeeping. However, many parishes expect more of them: They are recast as greeters—people who welcome regulars and visitors to the Mass. Very few priests try to usurp the role of usher during Mass. It would be counterproductive for the presider to abandon his chair to personally take up the collection each Sunday. The action would look more clerically venal than communally sacrificial. Instead, the priest entrusts the collection to others.

Nonetheless, when it comes to greeting people, a pastor can accomplish a lot by standing near the entrance, learning the names of those passing through the doors, and hearing the news from parishioners. He shares this duty with others, not in place of others. In many situations, especially in rural communities, the priest may personally greet everyone who walks in the door of a Catholic church.

A priest primarily interacts with these ministers during the Mass. When he diversifies these ministries among the greatest number of people, he encourages the participation of all. Whenever possible, one person does not perform two ministries, such as reader and usher, though sometimes it cannot be avoided. Less desirable is turning some of these responsibilities to the priest. He focuses on his own duties.

Giving Cues

Throughout the liturgy the priest communicates with ministers and the assembly. Depending on the circumstances, he connects ritually, subtly, or even frantically. His *ars celebrandi* will determine how.

In general, a priest presides well when he minimizes inessential comments. The fewer the words he adds, the more meaningful the words he uses.

Some unwanted, non-ritual conversations happen within the sanctuary. If a server or deacon asks an unexpected question mid-liturgy, it may shatter the focused intentionality of the priest's prayerful demeanor. Some questions and conversations become necessary due to unforeseen circumstances, but often they indicate something left unaddressed earlier. Questions are best handled before Mass begins.

Extraneous conversations have no place in the communion line. The communicant and the minister focus on the sacrament and the brief dialogue expressing faith in the Body and Blood of Christ. If the communicant has a pastoral need at home or a desire for information, that conversation belongs before or after Mass, not at the distribution of communion. If the priest realizes he needs a longer conversation with the communicant, a good *ars celebrandi* keeps him from saying something like, "See me after Mass." He has many ways of contacting people outside of Mass. The act of communion deserves respect.

Some priests give the faithful unnecessary instructions regarding posture. For example, after the collect some priests say, "Please be seated;" after the homily, "Please stand for the Creed;" and before the communion prayer; "Please stand."

People generally do not need these instructions. The regulars know what to do. When the presider tells them to do something they are already planning to do, he can make them feel infantilized, needlessly inferior, and obedient. Usually his own posture will indicate what they should do. When the priest sits, the people will sit. When he stands, they will as well. Letting them take control of their own posture energizes their participation.

Similarly, after the *Sanctus* a priest need not call out, "Please kneel." People are probably starting to do that, and this particular moment needs the presider's head focused on his prayer to the Father.

If the people need instruction, that task belongs first to the deacon. The deacon, not the priest, tells people about posture. If the people for some reason have not taken the correct posture, the subtlest solution is for the deacon to gesture what they should do: raising palms up to indicate standing; pushing palms down to indicate kneeling or sitting. If that does not work, as a last resort, the deacon gives the command with words. In the liturgy, however, words are like money. One does not spend them carelessly.

"Let us pray" does not mean "Please bring me the Missal," nor does it mean "Let us stand." At the collect, many priests announce the words "Let us pray" as if they really mean, "Server, please bring me the book." Many servers have learned not to move until they hear the words, "Let us pray," as if those words mean, "Let us pause while the server walks over here." Sometimes the words, "Let us pray" also seem to mean, "Let us wait another moment while I open the book to the correct page." Or even, "Let us wait yet another moment while I find the page I forgot to mark with a ribbon before Mass." The invitation to pray is meant to lead directly into prayer: silent, still prayer.

A prayerful *ars celebrandi* looks like this: At the time for the collect, the server brings the Missal to the priest. The priest opens it to the correct page. Then he says, "Let us pray," and without the distraction of any movement in the sanctuary, he observes silence while he actually prays. The presider unites his body language, his will, and his words. He shows the people that he is at prayer as he invites them into the presence of God.

Similarly, after communion, many priests observe silence when all has settled,[1] and then stand and announce, "Let us pray." They circumvent saying the words, "Please stand," but they intend it by their actions. Better is to be intentional, to link the words with the appropriate actions: to wait for the people to stand and then invite them to pray.

If the presider is consistent, the people will know how to respond. When he sits after the collect, they will sit. If he gives a clear introduction to the Our Father, the people will start the prayer with him. When he stands up after communion and waits, the people will stand. Cues can be subtle. As long as they are consistent, they will work.

Engaging the Faithful

The faithful are present to participate at Mass, just as the presider is. His duty is to engage them in the celebration. This symbiosis is evident from the Second Vatican Council's Constitution on the Sacred Liturgy cited above.

> Pastors of souls must, therefore, realize that, when the liturgy is celebrated, their obligation goes further than simply ensuring that the laws governing valid and lawful celebration are observed. They must also ensure that the faithful take part fully aware of what they are doing, actively engaged in the rite and enriched by it. (11)

Also, as indicated above, the GIRM addresses the priest's role in the eucharistic prayer in relationship to the people:

> The Priest calls upon the people to lift up their hearts towards the Lord in prayer and thanksgiving; he associates the people with himself in the Prayer that he addresses in the name of the entire community to God the Father through Jesus Christ in the Holy Spirit. (78)

He associates the people with himself. He guides them into the mystery of this celebration, helping them participate as well.

[1] OM 138 calls for a sacred silence "if appropriate" after communion.

Preparing the altar

The arrangement of elements on the altar tells the people something of the priest's intentions to associate them in the Mass. Pope Benedict XVI had his altar arranged with tall candles across the people's side. Other priests have followed his example. However, the Missal notes, "The candlesticks . . . should be appropriately placed . . . so that . . . the faithful may not be impeded from a clear view of what takes place at the altar or what is placed upon it" (GIRM 307). The altar does not belong to the priest alone. It belongs to the people as well. The priest faces the people not just to facilitate dialogues, but to gather the whole community around the common altar of sacrifice, at which the priestly people have a right and duty to exercise their ministry.

Pope Benedict also had placed on the altar a cross with an image of Christ facing him. It stood in addition to the crucifix already in the sanctuary. Every Mass is to be celebrated in the presence of an image of the crucified Christ (GIRM 117, 308). If there is no permanent crucifix in the sanctuary, then the processional cross remains in the sanctuary for the Mass, and "must be the only cross used" (GIRM 122) Many priests now place a crucifix on the altar as a focus of devotion. In the preconciliar Missal the priest looked at the cross during the opening of the Creed and just before giving the final blessing, so he had rubrics connecting him to the image. These were removed from the celebration in 1969. If two crosses occupy places in the sanctuary for Mass—one on the wall, for example, and another on the altar—the priest decides which one to face when he incenses the cross and the altar. If he incenses the cross on the wall, it looks as though the one on the altar is extraneous to the participation of the people at the same altar.

The placement of the Missal, missal stand, and vessels may also enhance or inhibit the participation of the people at the altar. In the preconciliar Mass, the missal stand and Missal rested to the side of center—sometimes the "epistle side" and sometimes the "gospel side." Today many priests still place the Missal and its stand to the side. It opens up their view to the congregation, helpful especially for the dialogues, but it also turns their head to the side for the most important words they say, the eucharistic prayer.

Some priests place the Missal flat on the altar without a stand, closest to themselves, and arrange the vessels on the other side of the Missal—the people's' side. This gives the people a better view of the bread and wine on the altar, and it lets the priest stand upright with a straight spine and neck as he extends his arms to pray.

The microphone

Many priests wear a portable microphone during the Mass to help the people hear. Sound amplification may be unnecessary in environments such as a chapel or rural church that seat a small number. Usually, however, a priest needs a mic. Even when he thinks he does not, everyone else may realize he does.

Some churches have separate microphones placed at the chair, ambo, and altar. In those situations a priest may not be wearing his own. These usually require no difficult instructions. A portable mic, however, needs greater attention to monitor the occasions when it is on and off.

People usually hear the amplified voice well if the presider avoids some common problems. If he wears the mic on the chasuble directly beneath his chin, it may not consistently pick up his voice, especially when he turns his head left and right. Sets worn over the ear avoid this problem by holding the mic in closer proximity to the presider's lips. The mic moves with his head and provides more consistency to the volume of his voice.

Two common problems are forgetting that the mic is on and leaving it on deliberately when it really could be switched off. If a priest leaves the mic on throughout the Mass, it picks up unintended sounds. It will broadcast his instructions to servers, his questions to the deacon, his coughs, the clearings of his throat, and every sigh he makes. During communion, it will pick up his dialogue with every single communicant. People may speak up about this, but many of them think it is impolite to correct a priest.

At other times the priest deliberately and injudiciously leaves the mic on so that his voice will predominate. This sometimes happens during congregational singing or the recitation of the Gloria and the Creed. When the congregation's voice should be heard, the presider's voice is but one among many. He presides by blending. He presides by holding a hymnal and singing—but not singing into a microphone. His voice on the mic may actually stifle others from singing or speaking. Leaving the microphone on is usually less helpful than many a priest thinks. It also communicates to the people a mixed message. Some of them may conclude, "He thinks we don't know how to read these words." Or, "He thinks we don't know what to do." A good *ars celebrandi* does not want to impede people's participation. It seeks to encourage it. Less is more. During moments of communal recitation and singing, when the presider turns down his personal volume, the volume of the people will usually increase.

Here is a sequence of microphone switches that the presider may consider:

Mic off: Opening hymn

Mic on: Sign of the cross

Mic off: Gloria

Mic on: Collect

Mic off: First reading

Mic on: Introducing the creed

Mic off: The creed

Mic on: Introducing the universal prayer

Mic off: The universal prayer

Mic on: Concluding the universal prayer

Mic off: Collection

Mic on: Preparation of the gifts

Mic off: Exchanging the sign of peace

Mic on: "Behold the Lamb of God"

Mic off: "Lord, I am not worthy"

Mic on: Prayer after communion

Mic off: Deacon's dismissal or closing hymn

By performing over a dozen switches during the course of the Mass, a presider can effectively let his solo voice resound, yet keep it from impeding the communal voice of the people. Now, if the microphone makes a noise every time, or if the priest visibly fumbles through his vestments to find the switch every time, he may simply speak softly when the mic is best off.

A priest may need to leave his mic on for the Lord's Prayer because of the gestures. He gives the invitation with hands joined, but then extends his hands immediately to begin the prayer. Switching the microphone off after "we dare to say" and back on again for "Deliver us" would require moving one's arms up and down twice, which would only distract people. The priest may be careful, however, to offer the Lord's Prayer in a low voice so that his does not override the sound of the assembly at prayer.

Eye contact

The priest will help everyone derive more meaning from the words he speaks if he maintains appropriate eye contact throughout the liturgy. He looks at the people when addressing them. He looks down at the Missal or up toward the heavens when addressing God. He looks at the reader for the readings. He avoids eye contact with the faithful while in procession, to avoid the impression that he merits the crowd's attention like a hero at a public parade.

The difference between the Gloria and the Creed illustrates this point. The Gloria is a hymn of praise to God. Consequently, the priest may look up to the heavens or down at the hymnal to take part. However, the Creed is a proclamation of faith to anyone who will listen. He may look directly at the congregation throughout the recitation of the Creed.

Similarly, in the words that follow the Lord's Prayer, the priest offers two prayers to God, and then addresses the people with a greeting of peace. After lifting his eyes up for the prayers, he may then take a moment to lower his eyes and look at the people he is about to address.

During the eucharistic prayer, the opening dialogue calls for direct eye contact with the people. The rubrics assign hand gestures to the presider, but no instructions concerning eyes. Opinions differ with the institution narrative and the words of consecration. Many priests look at the faithful while they say the words, "Take this, all of you." However, as shown above, he is praying to God the Father, not talking to the faithful. The nature of the words of institution implies no eye contact with the people.

Pauses

At times the presider may introduce a pause to give the people time to refocus. Especially when people are changing postures, they may need a moment to refocus their attention.

For example, after the *Sanctus*, when worshipers in the United States change from standing to kneeling, it takes them a few moments to assume their position. Often they make unintended noise while lowering kneelers, pushing belongings aside on the pew, or instructing children. Exercising a careful *ars celebrandi*, the presider waits until the room quiets down. He expects the people to pray along with him, and he cannot associate them with the eucharistic prayer until they have taken what time they need to get into position to concentrate.

After the eucharistic prayer, before beginning the Lord's Prayer, the people stand. This also requires time. Some presiders rush into the prayer but allowing time for the change in posture shows consideration for the needs of the people to prepare themselves to call upon the Father.

Later in the Mass, before hearing the prayer after communion, the people change their posture again. A thoughtful presider waits for the people to stand. It may take a moment. It may take some noise. When the room quiets down, he says, "Let us pray." He invites them to pray along. They cannot unless he first gives them some time.

The presider may introduce another pause not related to a change in posture to lengthen the space of time between the prayer over the offerings and the preface dialogue. Many priests press through these without a pause. Some silence can help people refocus. In the prayer over the offerings, they join the priest in prayer that God will accept the offerings that all have made. They answer amen to that prayer. In that prayer, all have directed their thoughts toward God. But in the very next line the priest speaks to the people ("The Lord be with you"), and they respond directly to the priest. All shift their intention from addressing God together to addressing each other in dialogue. A short pause, just enough to reestablish eye contact and new purpose, can enliven the preface dialogue.

Communal prayers

At certain points of the Mass the priest recites words together with the people. Most of these are prayers to God, though the Creed forms a notable exception.

The Missal suggests that the priest may introduce the Gloria. That is probably a blend of tradition and practicality. Somebody has to start it, and because it is a prayer to God during the introductory rites, the responsibility falls to the priest. In some musical settings, however, a cantor alone or all the people together begin this hymn and the priest joins the rest of the assembly.

Other parts of the Mass are also recited or sung by all: the *Confiteor*, the Creed, the Lord's Prayer and the Lamb of God. In many of these cases a skilled presider can involve the voice of the people together with him from the very first words.

With the *Confiteor*, it is nearly impossible for all to begin it together unless everyone knows that this is the option for the penitential act of the day's Mass and how long the silence preceding it will last. If there were a way for all to begin together the words, "I confess," that would be more powerful than hearing the priest alone make the first person declaration that belongs on the lips of every penitent member of the assembly. One possibility is for him to announce two words after the silence: "The *Confiteor*." Then after establishing eye contact with at least some of the faithful and taking a breath, he could begin "I confess" together with them. It engages the assembly more deliberately throughout the entire *Confiteor*.

For the Creed, a similar announcement can work to engage the entire congregation from the very beginning. The first two words are absolutely essential to proclaiming the Creed. In Latin, the single word *Credo* at the beginning is the only first-person singular verb in the entire profession of faith. Everything else follows from it. The English translation has everyone repeat the words "I believe" several times, mainly to facilitate comprehension. The Creed is so important as a personal and communal declaration of faith that the presider may consider engaging everybody's voice from the first word: "I." For example, he may hold a participation aid opened to the appropriate page and then announce, "The Nicene Creed." After pausing a moment and making eye contact with some of the people, he begins with them, "I believe." Something similar can be done when confessing the Apostles' Creed. Adding words to the Mass is a hazardous practice, but these are few, and they aim for a great value: to gain the people's voice at the very first word.

For the Lord's Prayer, people may easily begin together with the priest. They know it very well and they know when to start. They only require a pause that invites them to say the first words. These initial words hold special value again because of the first-person pronoun—in this case, "Our." Some priests say the first two words themselves, knowing that the people will catch up. However, those first words belong to them as well. This more complete engagement helps the participation of the people not just here but throughout the Mass. They learn that the presider values their voice, that he welcomes their initiative, and that he wants them active in the dialogues of the Mass.

The Lamb of God almost always needs someone to start it. If the musicians do not, then it falls to the priest or someone else, such as the reader. When possible, a cantor may begin it. The priest joins the singing while breaking the bread.

All these parts of the Mass are congregational, and the presider leads by sharing. He does not always need to say the first words. He does not need to leave his microphone on. The words belong to everyone. The priest can often engage the voice of the people by words that prompt, a face that invites, a pause, a breath, and a demeanor that expresses, "All together now." At times an active *ars celebrandi* leads in a way that invites leadership from the people as well.

Silences

The rubrics invite silence at several points of the Mass. The priest does not always have control over these. Nonetheless, if he is aware of the opportunities, he can help other ministers work with him to balance the silences and sounds of the Mass.

Silence precedes Mass. The Missal requests it in the church, sacristy, vesting room, and adjacent areas. Silence creates the proper disposition for carrying out the celebration "in a devout and fitting manner" (GIRM 45). In parishes, many priests use the time before Mass to visit with parishioners as they arrive and to consult pertinent ministers about various parts of the liturgy. A priest above all fittingly takes some time to collect himself before Mass. At the very least, before processing toward the altar, he can take a moment to recall what he is about to do and ask the Spirit to help all those responsible for celebrating this liturgy.

Some priests lead a short prayer with those ministers who will join the procession. Although not expected or required, the practice can naturally grow from the silence preceding Mass, unifying the ministers in their purpose.

The introduction to the penitential act invites the assembly to acknowledge their sins. People need time to do this. The person who speaks next may be the priest himself or a deacon who will lead the invocations of the third form of the penitential act. Either way, silence is key. Some nervous deacons presume that their cue to start the invocations is the moment the priest finishes his introduction. In truth, the Order of Mass calls for "a brief pause for silence" (OM 4). But a longer pause will get the attention of a people transitioning from the frenzy of life into reflective prayer. The presider especially takes sufficient time mentally to acknowledge his sins. A longer pause here will honor the gravity of the spiritual space that all have entered, schooling the faithful in the practice of examen. *Ars celebrandi* gives everyone time to reflect, people and priest.

After the words "Let us pray" a pause for silent prayer precedes the collect. Again it is "a brief silence," and it comes with two purposes: for the people to become aware of being in God's presence, and to recall their intentions (GIRM 54). Both these experiences require time. The silence after "Let us pray" summons people into God's presence as if entering the building, observing silence before Mass, and singing the opening song did not accomplish the goal. How much silence does that take? Probably more than what many priests allow. Outside the liturgy people become aware of God's presence in different ways, but silence is perhaps the most frequent. When the faithful are quiet, they hear God speak. In Psalm 24 the pilgrim people who enter Jerusalem's Temple pray for the king of Glory to enter with them. They do not presume that God is already there, but that they will experience the very entering of God in this holy space. After a presider says, "Let us pray," he is to leave enough time for that. Like anyone else in the culture, some priests are uncomfortable with silence, accustomed to noise and activity. The silence invites the presider to quiet his heart as well.

The second reason for this silence is for people to "call to mind their intentions" (GIRM 54). In many parishes, the last petition of the universal prayer goes something like this: "And for the special intentions we bring to Mass today." The Missal does not exclude such personal intentions at the universal prayer, but it does not promote them either (GIRM 70). The time it gives people to think about the special intentions they bring to Mass is at the silence that precedes the collect. Once their prayers fill the silence, the priest collects them. (That is one theory of the origin of the word "collect.") He gathers all these intentions and sums them up in the prayer he lifts on behalf of the people to God. If the presider is intentional about that purpose of the collect, the concluding "Amen" of the people will also sound intentional. All present have prayers they want God to hear. All need silence to recall them at this time.

Silence may characterize parts of the Liturgy of the Word. The Missal speaks eloquently about this:

> The Liturgy of the Word is to be celebrated in such a way as to favor meditation, and so any kind of haste such as hinders recollection is clearly to be avoided. In the course of it, brief periods of silence are also appropriate, accommodated to the assembled congregation; by means of these, under the action of the Holy Spirit, the Word of God may be grasped by the heart and a response through prayer may be prepared. (GIRM 56)

The same passage then recommends silences before the readings begin, after each of the first two readings, and at the conclusion of the homily. The purpose of all these is "to favor meditation." Few parishes accomplish all these.

The silence that precedes the first reading may be more practiced than people realize. There is almost always a gap between the amen that concludes the collect and the reader's announcement of the first reading. Ministers and people need time to sit. The reader needs time to approach the ambo. Once in place, the reader pauses to receive everyone's attention. One may not think of this as silence that favors meditation, but in a way it does.

The silences that follow the first and second readings, however, are rarer. The responsibility for managing these usually falls to the musicians or the reader. To gain allies in the quest for periods of silence during the Mass, the presider may start by conversing with these ministers outside of the liturgy. The one responsible for the responsorial psalm manages the silence that follows the first reading. If it is the one who just finished proclaiming the first reading, that person can invite silence by standing still at the ambo, personally meditating on the word he or she just read. If a psalmist is coming forward to the ambo to sing the responsorial, the change of ministers takes a moment of time. The purpose of that time is more spiritual than practical, however: It invites people to meditate.

The presider supports this practice when he fully engages his heart in the Liturgy of the Word. He listens attentively to the readings for his own benefit, a practice he can best model for others by watching the reader from his chair positioned in a way that facilitates this engagement. He then enters the silences through thoughtful meditation, head down, eyes closed.

Silence after the homily lets people reflect on the preacher's words. The very recommendation challenges preachers to say something worthy of immediate reflection. After preaching, some homilists welcome silence because they just want a break. They have worked hard on their presentation, so when they finish sharing their heart through preaching, they need to take a breath. Observing silence seated at the chair can help a presider relax and refocus.

The people make a silent preparation for their own communion while the priest recites his quiet prayer of preparation (GIRM 84). Many priests offer this prayer during the Lamb of God. The presider has two quiet prayers here, one that accompanies the commingling and the other that prepares for his communion. Although many priests offer these back-to-back, the first is said during the Lamb of God, but the second is appointed after it (GIRM 129, 130, 131). The priest encourages the silent preparation of the people when he says his own prayer of preparation quietly *after* all have finished the Lamb of God.

Silence may follow communion (OM 138, GIRM 43, 45, 88, 164). Unlike the collect, which invites the assembly to observe silence in order to become aware of the presence of God and to recall intentions, the liturgy calls for silence after communion for all to "praise God in their hearts and pray to him" (GIRM 45). Priests, too, may use this time for the same purpose. They may have other responsibilities: returning a ciborium to the tabernacle or purifying vessels. Yet even while performing these duties, he can use the silence to "praise God" and "pray to him." He probably does this already without thinking.

The prayer after communion follows this period of silence. Once the priest says, "Let us pray," the Missal gives some practical, often overlooked advice: "All pray in silence with the Priest for a while, unless silence has just been observed" (OM 139). The presider introduces this prayer in the same way as the collect, but the similarity may end there. For the prayer after communion, the silence after the words "Let us pray" is optional. For example, if people have been singing throughout the distribution of communion and the cleansing of vessels, they all may need some silence after hearing "Let us pray." But otherwise, the people and the priest may all have observed their period of silence during the reposition of the communion hosts and the cleansing of vessels. Consequently, after the priest says, "Let us pray," he may proceed without pause directly to the prayer. People need time to praise God and pray to him, as the Missal observes, but if that has happened, the presider may move on. Often the rest of the assembly has already enjoyed more silence than he has. He need not introduce more silence after "Let us pray" if the people have already been praying.

Disturbances

Interactions between the priest, ministers, and people are usually intentional, purposeful, and even scripted. Presiders communicate with other ministers, and they style their engagement with the faithful through words, gestures, and silences. However, every so often, something else happens. Some disturbance occurs—something that the liturgical books never envisioned. Such activity upsets the purpose of the liturgy. But in the real world, disturbances happen.

For example, at a wedding, a photographer enters the sanctuary for a close shot of the couple's exchange of consent. During the first reading, a member of the faithful talks at full volume on a cellphone. During the homily, a toddler runs into the sanctuary. During the eucharistic prayer an elderly woman in a pew has a medical emergency requiring imminent assistance.

Even those lightly experienced in the liturgy could add more examples. All around the world priests can recount unexpected distractions to their liturgies.

When one of these happens, a presider focused on presiding has to make a decision regarding the intensity of his response. One approach is to ask the question, "Which would cause more distraction: allowing the disturbance to continue or stopping it?"

If allowing the disturbance to continue seems less disruptive, the presider may continue with the Mass. Clearly, an infant suddenly wailing in its mother's arms does not require the presider's intervention. Tolerating the infant contributes to the prayerful spirit of the liturgy. When the presider concentrates on the prayers at hand, his composure messages the parents that the child's behavior does not matter in the great scheme of things. He conveys gratitude that the parents brought the child to Mass. The parents do their part; the presider does his.

The more difficult judgments come from circumstances ranging from photographers to emergency personnel. The infractions of some photographers seem minor, even when they focus on commemorating the event more than on praying at the same occasion. At other times, however, a photographer disrupts the ceremony, and the presider may need to disrupt further to give them the rules they should have learned beforehand. Then the priest returns to presiding. Such an incident can severely break a presider's spiritual center, turning him into the inappropriate role of law enforcement rather than sacrificial priest. If a deacon or ushers are present, they more fittingly take the responsibility for addressing those who disturb. But if no one else is helping, the presider may interrupt the proceedings to deal with the problem. The basic question returns: "Which would cause more distraction: allowing the disturbance to continue or stopping it?"

Many Masses are live-streamed, and special events are recorded for posterity, whether by professional photographers or cellphone-equipped congregants. However the presider responds to disturbances, his actions may be shared broadly on social media before the end of the Mass. His choices may be widely critiqued.

Ars celebrandi encourages the presider to think before interrupting the liturgy. As much as possible, he stays inside his guiding role as the liturgy asks him to do.

A good presider does not cause disturbances. Yet sometimes the priest himself is the guilty party. Some priests and deacons pull out *their* cellular devices during a liturgy to snap a photo of a moment they wish to remember. Whether ministering at a confirmation with the bishop, a wedding anniversary, or a baptism, a priest best leaves his camera alone.

Through all of these interactions a priest refines his *ars celebrandi*. He remains focused on his particular role, fully engaged in the liturgy as it was prepared and fully creative to handle disturbances that may beset any Mass.

When Abraham sealed the covenant with the Lord, God asked him to offer up a heifer, a goat, a ram, a turtledove, and a young pigeon (Gen 15:9). Abraham got them, split them (except for the birds), and neatly arranged them. Then, in one of the biblical verses most consoling to people responsible for executing a well-ordered liturgy, Genesis says that birds swooped down on the carcasses, and Abram scared them away (Gen 15:11). Not everything will go according to plan, no matter how faithfully one strives to execute the rubrics. Like Abraham, a priest may interrupt even the most solemn, historical moment due to forces beyond his control. When the presider keeps his head, he makes a sacrifice worthy of God.

6

Overlooked Rubrics

All priests overlook some rubrics that plainly stare back at them from the Missal. Once a priest establishes a pattern of presiding, he stays with what works. The same repetitious character of the Mass that makes it boring to young people makes it attractive to a priest. He derives deeper layers of meaning and spiritual satisfaction every time he returns to these mysteries.

Therefore, changing behaviors never comes easy. It exacts a price. Yet the rewards can be huge. Sometimes even a slight adjustment can make a priest more aware of his task at any given moment. If he listens humbly to criticism and receives the perspective of others with an open ear, he can learn more about himself and hear God's call in new ways. Often the rubrics ask for something that a priest thinks cannot be a good idea. If he tries it, however, he may discover that it is.

Many priests overlook the rubrics selected for the following section. Those who are surprised by them are not alone. Each priest may discover that making a change increases fidelity to the liturgy, a benefit to him and inspiration to the people who join him at prayer.

Specific Parts of the Mass

Antiphons

The Missal assigns two antiphons for each celebration: one at the entrance and the other at communion. On days when musicians have prepared for these parts of the Mass, the song of the people replaces the antiphons for the day. If there is no music, however, then the antiphons have to be accounted for. Several options avail. At the entrance, the antiphon "is recited either by the faithful, or by some of them, or by a reader; otherwise, it is recited by the Priest himself, who may even adapt it as an introductory explanation" (GIRM 48).

Those who have a copy of the antiphon may recite it together. If copies are scarce, the reader for the Mass may speak it alone. As a last resort, the priest recites it before making the sign of the cross (GIRM 50).

In the final option the priest may adapt the words of the antiphon as an introductory explanation. In that case, he begins with the sign of the cross, greets the people, and then refers to the antiphon in the Missal to inspire his introduction to the Mass.

The second edition of the Order of Celebrating Matrimony (OCM) offers a model. Enhancing the 2016 English translation is a scripted introduction for the priest. He was always permitted to make an introduction, but now the OCM gives him two options to consider. He need not use either one, but he may. Or he may study them as models for his own introduction.

Catholic weddings usually begin with an organ solo, not with a congregational hymn. They may begin with a hymn, as far as the OCM is concerned, but usually not as far as the families and friends are concerned. They envision instrumental music. If the wedding takes place at Mass, however, the entrance antiphon needs to be accounted for. If the people did not sing a hymn, then one of the other options in GIRM 48 applies.

Apparently, the writer of the OCM's second sample introduction preempted this concern by adopting the idea of incorporating the antiphon. The first of the Missal's three possible entrance antiphons at a wedding Mass comes from Psalm 20: "May the Lord send you help from the holy place and give you support from Sion. May he grant you your hearts' desire and fulfill every one of your designs."[1] The second sample introduction for a wedding Mass has the priest conclude his opening address to the couple with these words: "May the Lord hear you on this your joyful day. May he send you help from heaven and protect you. May he grant you your hearts' desire and fulfill every one of your prayers" (OCM 53). This provides a simple example of how the presider may incorporate the entrance antiphon at any Mass that does not begin with congregational singing.

At Sunday Mass, some cathedrals and parishes have a choir sing the day's Gregorian chant introit before the opening hymn. GIRM 48 does not envision starting Mass with two versions of the entrance antiphon. Singing the introit preserves the chant tradition, and perhaps it serves as a prelude to the Mass while the opening hymn serves as the proper entrance chant accompanying the procession. Ideally, though, Mass begins with only one antiphon or hymn. Similarly, it would not be appropriate for the priest to read the antiphon at a Mass when everyone has just sung an opening hymn together.

At communion, "if there is no singing, the antiphon given in the Missal may be recited either by the faithful, or by some of them, or by a reader; otherwise, it is recited by the Priest himself after he has received Communion and before he distributes Communion to the faithful" (GIRM 87). Here the Missal offers no option for paraphrasing the antiphon into remarks, and wisely so. The act of communion is underway. All the focus is there. Ideally, singing covers the entire act of communion. The purpose of this antiphon is "to express the spiritual union of the communicants by means of the unity of their voices, to show gladness of heart, and to bring out more clearly the 'communitarian' character of the procession to receive the Eucharist. The singing is prolonged for as long as the Sacrament is being administered to the faithful" (GIRM 86). Singing, then, expresses meanings and supplies benefits to communion.

If there is no singing, however, then one of the other options applies. When the people recite these antiphons together, it unifies their voices before communion, unites their hearts with one another and

[1] Roman Missal, Ritual Masses, For the Celebration of Marriage, A.

with Christ. Failing that, one other person may recite the antiphon. But if it falls to the priest, the antiphon slips in between his communion and that of the people. Singing ideally begins when the priest receives communion so that one song covers the communion of the entire assembly (OM 136, GIRM 86, 159). Without music, it would seem improper for the priest himself to read the communion antiphon between "Lord, I am not worthy" and his own private preparation and reception. So the antiphon is delayed until he has completed his communion.

In short, the priest practicing good *ars celebrandi* ensures that both antiphons are recited at Masses without music—even at daily Mass.

Blessing and sprinkling of water

On Sundays, as an alternative to the penitential act, the priest may conduct the blessing and sprinkling of water. The ceremony used to appear more obviously together with the options for the penitential act in the Order of Mass, but the third edition of the Roman Missal has moved the ritual into an appendix because of its location in the original Latin language edition of the Missal. A footnote in the Order of Mass tells the priest where to find it.

The blessing and sprinkling of water is recommended for Easter Time, but it may be celebrated on any Sunday of the year. Sunday celebrates the resurrection of Christ. Baptism extends a preliminary share in his divine life. The blessing and sprinkling of water, then, reminds the faithful of their baptism and of the resurrection, which they commemorate each Sunday.

This ceremony may be rotated with the options for the penitential act. That way, the people experience the various ways of celebrating the introductory rites that the liturgical reforms richly shared with them. On a practical note, the priest could lead this ceremony whenever the parish's reservoir of holy water runs low. Instead of blessing the water privately and simply, the priest may bless a quantity at the beginning of one Sunday Mass.

The second form of the penitential act is rarely used because many congregations have never learned the responses. As with any other form of prayer, they require repetition. The presider may more successfully use the second form several times a week at daily Mass, for example, because the stable group present there can learn it well. On Sundays it may be better to use the second form consistently for a period of weeks; for example, on the Sundays of Lent or in the last months of Ordinary Time. People then can practice from Sunday to Sunday and gradually learn the responses.

In this second form of the penitential act, the Kyrie or "Lord, have mercy" comes after the prayer of absolution, "May almighty God have mercy on us," just as it does in the first form, the *Confiteor* ("I confess to almighty God"). It is not to be omitted.

The sign of peace

Some priests are most aware, others are unaware that the sign of peace is optional. The Order of Mass says, "Then, if appropriate, the Deacon, or the Priest, adds: Let us offer each other sign of peace" (OM 128). One could ask, "Well, when would it not be appropriate to express peace?" Indeed. Many dioceses called for its exclusion during the COVID-19 pandemic; however, the sign of peace can be exchanged without touching. If societies, families, or ecclesial bodies polarize, this sign reinforces a foundation of charity.

The same paragraph of the Order of Mass explains the purpose of the sign of peace. Only rarely do the rubrics do this. For example, explanations accompany the silence after "Let us pray" at the collect and for the inclusion of the universal prayer at Mass. In this case, the rubric says that the sign "expresses peace, communion, and charity." It is the first of the signs of communion, pointing toward sacramental communion. The sign of peace is not the time for people to introduce themselves, nor for the priest to catch someone's attention for a purpose foreign to the Eucharist underway. It is not a time for making peace; that is, it is not a time for reconciliation. It is a sign that "expresses peace," the peace that already reigns among Christians gathered for the Mass.

The Order of Celebrating Matrimony omits the words "if appropriate." Apparently a sign of peace is always appropriate and expected at a wedding Mass.

The priest gives the sign of peace "to a Deacon or minister" (OM 128). The liturgy does not expect him to go further into the assembly. In some ethnically based communities, the sign of peace takes on a life of its own, and a priest who does not join in the spirit of the moment may unwillingly send a message of disinterest in peace. Ordinarily, though, he stays at or near the altar and exchanges peace with those nearby. A priest who likes to shake too many hands at this point of the Mass may ask himself, "Is this a sign of the importance of peace? Or a sign of the importance of me?"

The breaking of the bread

At the Lamb of God the priest breaks the host into several parts. Before saying, "Behold the Lamb of God," he "takes the host" and raises it above the paten or chalice (OM 132).

The Missal says a little more about what is expected of him at this time, however. In the section called "The Bread and Wine for Celebrating the Eucharist," the GIRM requires that the bread "truly have the appearance of food," and that it "be fashioned in such a way that the Priest at Mass with the people is truly able to break it into parts and distribute these to at least some of the faithful." By doing so, he brings out "more clearly the force and importance of the sign of the unity of all in the one bread, and of the sign of charity by the fact that the one bread is distributed among the brothers and sisters" (GIRM 321).

The priest is to break the bread and distribute its parts to some of the faithful. This applies even to a three-inch host. He breaks it in order to share it. This shows unity: all are one in the one bread. And it shows charity: the priest shares his bread with others.

Many priests break and completely consume the presider's host, however. This action lacks the symbols of unity and charity that GIRM 321 has in mind.

Some priests break the host in two, then break off a smaller part from one half, and place that part into the chalice as the rubrics direct. However, some priests then reassemble the other broken parts of the host into a circle, using thumb and forefinger to conceal the missing part they put into the chalice. They lift up to the view of the faithful what looks like an unbroken host over the chalice—as if to make them wonder, "How did he do that?" This establishes the visual image of a host floating over a chalice, so popular in Catholic iconography, but a juxtaposition of elements completely misrepresents the purpose of the breaking of bread.

A better practice is to share. Some large presider's hosts break into twenty-four pieces, most suitable for sharing. If using a three-inch host, the presider breaks it into four pieces and then break off another small piece for the chalice. For "Behold the Lamb of God," he raises a broken host, the quarter that he plans to consume. After receiving the host and drinking from the chalice, he then shares the other three broken pieces with some communicants. In this tiny way he symbolizes the unity and charity that the Eucharist fosters.

A priest may also consider whether the use of a separate paten and chalice for his communion interferes with the same values of unity and charity. Eating from a shared paten and drinking from a shared chalice may better express the purposes of communion.

Communion from the tabernacle

The people participate most fully when they receive communion from hosts consecrated at the same Mass. A priest is required to receive the same way—including a concelebrant. But at a typical parish Mass almost anywhere around the world, about the time of the Lamb of God, the priest, deacon, or a communion minister goes to the tabernacle, genuflects, opens the door, removes the ciborium, carries it to the altar, sets it down, and removes the lid. At communion time, at least one minister will distribute communion to the people from those hosts. Most people do not seem to mind. They came to Mass for communion, and they care not whether it comes from the tabernacle or the altar. But the Missal takes another view:

> It is most desirable that the faithful, just as the Priest himself is bound to do, receive the Lord's Body from hosts consecrated at the same Mass and that, in the cases where this is foreseen, they partake of the chalice (cf. no. 283), so that even by means of the signs Communion may stand out more clearly as a participation in the sacrifice actually being celebrated. (GIRM 85)

This practice stems from the council's view that the full, conscious, active participation of the people is the aim to be considered above all else. Participation is more than postures and gestures, dialogues and acclamations. It also pertains to the reception of communion. As the priestly people who give thanks to God and offer sacrifice, they also receive communion—as the priestly people. As the ordained priest receives communion from the offerings of the same Mass, so the lay faithful are encouraged to do the same.

The first obstacle to overcome is the opinion, "What difference does it make?" If it made no difference, then the priest could receive communion from the tabernacle as well. For Holy Thursday's Mass of the Lord's Supper, the liturgy begins with an empty tabernacle.[2] No one receives previously consecrated hosts at that Mass. At least on that night once a year the church asks all the priestly people to participate fully by receiving communion from the bread consecrated in the same Mass. To offer less on any other day of the year diminishes the full participation of the people.

Most priests could arrange this fairly easily at weekday masses following one of two different ways. In the first, the sacristan sets bread and wine at the end of the aisle away from the altar, in position for the procession of the gifts. The number of hosts matches the number anticipated for Mass, but the sacristan keeps a reserve supply adjacent to the vessels. Before the procession of the gifts—perhaps during the universal prayer—the sacristan adjusts the host count by adding a few more from the supply or transferring the excess from the ciborium.

A second way puts the responsibility on the priest. If he expects between twelve and twenty-four communicants, he may use one large host that can be broken into twenty-four pieces. At the breaking of the bread, he counts the number of communicants in the assembly and breaks the host accordingly. For example, he may break it into sixteen pieces, leaving eight of them double in size. If the number of communicants regularly approaches forty-eight people, he may use two large hosts in the same way.

Near the end of communion, a priest may discover that the count is short or that more participants arrived late. In that case, he breaks the last few. If a miscount produces a few hosts too many, he may give communion to the last communicant, bring the remaining few hosts to the altar and consume them there, with or without the help of others.

[2] Roman Missal, Thursday of the Lord's Supper, at the Evening Mass, 5.

With careful planning, a priest need rarely use the tabernacle for daily Mass. He begins the Liturgy of the Eucharist with a sufficient number of hosts, and communion concludes with all of them consumed. All the priestly people receive communion from the bread consecrated at that Mass. This gives the Mass a more complete feel—everyone has fully taken part in the same sacrifice.

On Sundays the challenge is greater but not insurmountable. The same strategies can be invoked. A good sacristan can count the participants and adjust the supply of hosts to be carried to the altar in the procession of the gifts. Or the sacristan can bring several large hosts, all of which can be divided into twenty-four pieces. The priest breaks them accordingly. Adjusting the number is a challenge, but it can be done.

More people then fruitfully come to see the altar as the source of their communion. As it is, many Catholics see the tabernacle this way. If no communion rite begins without a trip to the tabernacle, people continuously observe that the priest receives communion from the altar, and they receive theirs from the tabernacle. Even if only some of them receive from the tabernacle, the distinction is not well noted. Many of the people have not yet learned the significance and expectation of their full participation.

Objection may come from sacristans who insist that feeding everyone from the bread consecrated at the same Mass cannot be done. Some of them fret over a tabernacle's ciborium when it is too full. Or they fret over a ciborium too empty. By implication they wrongly perceive that one purpose of the Mass is to manage the supply of hosts in the tabernacle.

In truth, every so often the tabernacle is too full or too empty. At times the sacristan misjudges the number of hosts needed. At Masses where sacristans have underestimated the required number, ministers will indeed distribute from the tabernacle to the last communicants. At times, the sacristan reports a legitimate concern: The number of hosts reserved in the tabernacle is excessive. Then, the priest may justifiably distribute communion from the tabernacle even to all the faithful at all the Masses that weekend in order to handle the situation. He may need to do that once every month or more. But not at every single Mass.

Blessing in the communion line

In many parishes some of the faithful who are not receiving communion join the procession anyway. When they reach the front, they cross their arms to indicate that they will not be receiving communion that day. They seek a blessing instead. Many people find this welcoming. Some liturgists find it appalling.

There is virtually no legislation on this—nothing official from the Vatican, nor from the USCCB. A given diocese may issue directives, or a priest may have established some in his parish. But one searches in vain for any official rubric or instruction to help in this matter.

Some of those in line are children too young for their First Communion, non-Catholics present at the invitation of a Catholic, or Catholics who for whatever reason feel unworthy of receiving communion.

In 2008 the CDWDS sent a private letter (Protocol No. 930/08/L) on the topic, observing several points: the liturgical blessing at the end of Mass follows communion in a matter of minutes; laypeople such as extraordinary ministers of holy communion may not confer blessings within Mass; hand laying has another significance and should be discouraged; pastors cannot perform ceremonies for invalidly remarried persons (*Familiaris Consortio*, n. 84); Catholics under penalties in canon 915 and non-Catholics should neither approach communion nor receive a blessing.[3] This private letter does not constitute an official statement, so it has no legislative force.

By contrast, in 2014, rewriting his conclusion to an article from 1972, Pope Emeritus Benedict XVI endorsed the practice of having noncommunicants ask

> for a blessing, which is given to them as a sign of the love of Christ and of the Church. This form could certainly be chosen also by persons who are living in a second marriage and therefore are not admitted to the Lord's table. The fact that this would make possible an intense spiritual communion with the Lord, with his whole Body, with the Church, could be a spiritual experience that would strengthen and help them.[4]

[3] Turner, *Let Us Pray*, p. 146.

[4] Quoted in Sandro Magister, "In the Synod on the Family Even the Pope Emeritus Is Speaking Out" (December 3, 2014), http://chiesa.espresso.repubblica.it/articolo/1350933bdc4.html?eng=y.

Even so, the reasons shared by the CDWDS in its private letter of 2008 deserve reflection. Communion is not a time for blessing, nor should communion be equated with blessing. They are just not the same. There is a very nice blessing at the end of Mass, as the CDWDS indicates, and it really counts. If people stay for the end, they receive this blessing. The forgoing prayers and actions of the Mass are building up to the communion of the faithful, and the addition of blessing for noncommunicants at this time dilutes the significance of the ceremony. The communion rite is not about welcoming. Welcoming happens much earlier. Communion concerns communion.

Even though the practice has problems, many priests accommodate it. If someone shows up in the communion line with arms crossed, they don't send them back unacknowledged. One strategy is to take the thumb of the hand not used to distribute communion and trace a sign of the cross on the person's forehead. This is the same gesture performed at the baptism of a child, which even parents and godparents may imitate. Consequently, this gesture cannot fall into the category of blessings at Mass forbidden to lay people to administer. To avoid any physical contact, a simple bow of the head may suffice to acknowledge the presence of the non-communicant.

Nearly every priest has his own idea of what to do. There is no easy solution. Caution is advised. Some priests want all those requesting a blessing to enter their line, but this seems excessive. Lay communion ministers could surely acknowledge the noncommunicant. Making a public announcement inviting noncommunicants to come forward with arms crossed also seems excessive because no liturgical foundation for the practice exists.

No resolution to this dilemma seems forthcoming. No matter what the authorities say, they face opposition. If they ask noncommunicants to remain in their pew, which indeed makes the most liturgical sense, they will be accused of maltreating visitors and young children. If they invite people forward for a blessing, they invite accusations of distorting the purpose of communion.

Some priests speak words of blessing to noncommunicants. However, as mentioned above, during the liturgy, words are like money. They are best conserved. One does not spend what one does not have. If the liturgical books give no words to say, then it is hard to justify expressions such as, "May God bless you," "May Jesus reign in your heart," or "May Christ come to you this day." The least disruptive solution may be some acknowledgment of the person's presence, saying nothing.

Announcements

Parish announcements are to be made after the prayer after communion, not before (OM 140, GIRM 90a, 166, 184). In some parishes, the announcements incorrectly take place after communion while everyone is seated quietly. Misreading this as everyone seated waiting, some priests leap into the void with announcements so that no one is bored. But this silence has a purpose—spending time in communion with Christ whom all have just received.

Whenever the liturgical rubrics speak about announcements, they characterize them with two descriptors: brief, and only those that are necessary.[5]

Additionally, the introduction to the *Lectionary for Mass* says that "Any necessary announcements are to be kept completely separate from the homily; they must take place following the prayer after Communion."[6] In the past some priests customarily began the homily with announcements to accommodate those who arrived late for Mass and those who left early. Now the governing criterion is the liturgical sense.

The announcements fit more with the concluding rites than with the communion rite. The prayer after communion brings the action of communion to a close. It seals everything that has been building since the Lord's Prayer. Then the liturgy turns its attention to getting people back to their lives. This starts with announcements about what is happening in the parish in the coming week, ways that people can share the gospel, learn their faith, join in prayer, or build up the Body of Christ through socialization. The announcements are preparing for the dismissal. They remind people what specifically they may do when they go in peace to love and serve the Lord.

[5] OM 140, GIRM 90a, 166, 184. Yes, all four citations.

[6] Introduction to the *Lectionary for Mass*, 27.

Solemn blessings and prayers over the people

The presider may extend the final blessing by offering a solemn blessing or a prayer over the people. The first is addressed to the people, the second to God.

The Missal locates these in the pages that follow the Order of Mass. The Order of Mass itself says that the greeting and its response precede the more solemn formula of blessing (OM 142). Then the deacon or, in his absence, the priest commands, "Bow down for the blessing." The complete sequence goes like this:

Priest: The Lord be with you.

The people: And with your spirit.

Deacon [or priest]: Bow down for the blessing.

Priest: [solemn blessing or prayer over the people.]

The people: Amen. [three times or once]

Priest: May almighty God bless you. . . .

The people: Amen.

Deacon [or priest]: Go forth, the Mass is ended [or another dismissal formula]

The people: Thanks be to God.

Some priests misunderstand how the complete formula flows. They omit the greeting, or they omit the command to bow for the blessing. Some mix up the sequence. The formula above, however, shows what the Missal intends.

The solemn blessing has three parts; the people answer "Amen" to each. Often, the response is weak. The same seasonal variety that makes these blessings appealing produces diverse phrasal endings that do not naturally elicit that "Amen" with a clear cue. Several strategies may ameliorate the situation.

The presider may sing the phrases. Music for the solemn blessing can be found near the end of the Missal's first appendix. If a congregation can learn how to sing "Amen," and if the presider can learn the tones for the threefold blessing, this solution may be appealing. The sung cadence at the end of each phrase clearly cues the people to sing "Amen."

If speaking the three parts of the blessing, the presider may help the people find their way if he both modulates his voice and changes the position of his hands. As he reaches the end of each phrase, he slows down and chooses a vocal range that communicates to the people, "That is it. It's your turn." Then, because he has raised his arms over them to speak each part, he visibly moves his arms down each time to elicit their response.

Repetition builds confidence. The presider will help the people anticipate their response if he uses a solemn blessing every week for a few months. The people will catch on. The repetition of solemn blessings builds the people's confidence.

The prayer over the people is addressed to God. A careful presider will adjust the direction of his eyes accordingly. He looks at the people for the solemn blessing because he is addressing them, but for a prayer *over* the people he looks up or down to the place he usually directs his eyes when addressing any of the Missal's prayer to God.

The congregation usually responds well to a prayer over the people because it ends with a familiar phrase that signals their "Amen." Even so, singing the prayer and the blessing may provide a pleasing conclusion to the Mass.

During Lent the Missal assigns a prayer over the people for each day. On weekdays these may be omitted, or they may be exchanged. For example, if the presider prefers Wednesday's prayer over the people for Monday's Mass, he may use it instead.

On Sundays of Lent, however, the prayers over the people are obligatory as they appear in the Missal. Centuries ago the liturgy included such prayers to help mark the penitential season of Lent. They fell out of custom but returned in English with the 2011 Missal. They pace the season with a special feature.

These prayers reach a climax at the Good Friday celebration of the Passion of the Lord. Although the rubrics are not clear, the presider probably does not say, "The Lord be with you" before the prayer over the people on Good Friday. The same greeting is missing from the introductory rites and from the proclamation of the passion that day. The omission implies that the Lord is not "with you" in the usual way on Good Friday when the church commemorates his death. Therefore, the greeting is abandoned for the prayer over the people on that single day.

Incidentally, the previous English translation had the deacon or priest say, "Bow your heads and pray for God's blessing." It also permitted the minister to use those or similar words. The present Missal made two changes here. One is in the translation. The Latin never said "Bow your heads." It just commanded people to bow. It implies that they bow from the waist. Second, the third edition of the Missal removed the opportunity to use these or similar words. The 2011 English translation incorporated the change.

Recurring Elements in the Mass

In addition to the overlooked rubrics in those specific parts of the Mass, others concern recurring elements of the Mass. These routine elements may receive inadequate attention. Often the details conceal a deep meaning. When strung together with care, they can create a tapestry of insight into the Eucharist.

Genuflections and bows

Reverences occur throughout the Mass (GIRM 274, 275). Each type signifies the importance of the object or person receiving the genuflection or bow.

A genuflection is reserved for the Most Blessed Sacrament. During the Triduum, a genuflection is made to the cross from its appearance in the Good Friday liturgy until the beginning of the Easter Vigil. More solemn than a bow, a genuflection is reserved for the most sacred objects of devotion.

Because of the belief that Christ is truly present in the Eucharist, the priest genuflects twice during the consecration and once more before receiving communion. At the beginning and the end of Mass, the ministers genuflect to the tabernacle if it is located in the sanctuary. If it is not, as is the case at St. Peter's Basilica in Rome, for example, then the priest and other ministers make no genuflection at the beginning and end of Mass. The apposite rubric includes another important detail:

> If, however, the tabernacle with the Most Blessed Sacrament is situated in the sanctuary, the Priest, the Deacon, and the other

> ministers genuflect when they approach the altar and when they depart from it, but not during the celebration of Mass itself. (GIRM 274)

Those last few words assist a critical understanding of the purpose of the tabernacle, the meaning of the Mass, and the centrality of the altar during the celebration. If the tabernacle is in the sanctuary—against the back wall, for example—the ministers in procession genuflect when they arrive at the sanctuary at the beginning of Mass and again when they leave the sanctuary at the end. During the Mass, however, when ministers pass from one side of the sanctuary to the other, they do *not* genuflect to the tabernacle. Instead, according to the *Ceremonial of Bishops* (CB), they make a profound bow to the altar: "A deep bow is made to the altar by all who enter the sanctuary . . ., leave it, or pass before the altar."[7]

During the course of the Mass, the liturgy focuses on the altar of sacrifice. Genuflections acknowledge the real presence of Christ in the tabernacle at the beginning and end of the service, but during the Mass the community's attention shifts to the altar. That is where the bread and wine will become the Body and Blood of Christ, and that is the table from which communion is shared. Therefore, *during* the Mass, servers crossing from one side of the sanctuary to the other bow to the altar, not the tabernacle; ushers walking to the front pew for the collection bow to the altar instead of genuflecting; readers and communion ministers entering or leaving the sanctuary bow to the altar.

At the beginning and end of Mass, even when the tabernacle is in the sanctuary, ministers carrying the processional cross or candles neither genuflect nor make a profound bow for obvious reasons (GIRM 274). They merely bow their heads to keep the cross upright and dignified, and to protect the servers from spilling wax on the floor.

If a priest or other minister is unable to perform a genuflection, common sense permits a bow instead. In general, however, it is not appropriate to bow to the Blessed Sacrament, whether in the tabernacle or during the Liturgy of the Eucharist. The Blessed Sacrament receives a genuflection.

[7] ICEL, *Ceremonial of Bishops* (Collegeville, MN: Liturgical Press, 1989), 72.

The Missal is silent about genuflecting to the tabernacle before and after communion when retrieving previously consecrated hosts and reposing those that remain. It seems inappropriate to genuflect to the tabernacle when retrieving the hosts because there are already consecrated hosts on the altar. When reposing the remaining hosts, however, in keeping with the practice at the end of the Mass of the Lord's Supper on Holy Thursday, the minister places the hosts in the tabernacle, genuflects, and then closes the door.[8] If a deacon or another minister reposes the hosts, there is no rubric calling for the priest to stand and watch. The absence of such a rubric demonstrates the liturgy's commitment to the sacrifice of the Mass and the communion of the faithful, rather than on acts of devotion.

Bows are not as reverential as a genuflection, but they signify "reverence and honor shown to the persons themselves or to the signs that represent them" (GIRM 275). There are two kinds of bows, according to GIRM 275, which then proceeds to distinguish three of them. The bow of the head and the bow of the body (the profound bow) are the two main kinds. The priest bows slightly for the words of consecration, creating a third type of bow.

The head bow is made for certain names: "when the three Divine Persons are named together and at the names of Jesus, of the Blessed Virgin Mary, and of the Saint in whose honor Mass is being celebrated" (GIRM 275a). This rubric is in the passive voice, so it is not clear who is supposed to bow the head. Presumably, it is the person who speaks these names, usually the priest. However, it does not exclude the people from bowing their heads when they pronounce such names in the Creed, for example, or even when they hear the priest pronounce them. Many Catholic parents instructed their children to bow their head at the name of Jesus. The Missal agrees, and it adds several more names.

Therefore, the presider bows his head when making the sign of the cross at the start of Mass and when giving the final blessing at the end, for example. It also means that any mention of Mary's name comes with a head bow, whether during the Creed or in the eucharistic prayer—or in the *Confiteor*. The saint of the day is usually mentioned in the collect, sometimes in the other presidential prayers, and

[8] Roman Missal, Mass of the Lord's Supper, 39.

sometimes in the preface. If the saint of the day is mentioned in the eucharistic prayer, whether inserted into Prayer III or present already in Prayer I, then the name receives a head bow on that day. This simple gesture, much ignored by many presiders, can make the priest more conscious of the sacredness of the very names of the Trinity whom Christians adore and of the saints whom they venerate.

In the United States the bishops have added a bow of the head as the sign of reverence when receiving communion. When people approach in line, each of them is to bow his or her head to the sacrament before receiving it (GIRM 160). Communicants do not consistently implement this request. When their turn comes to receive, some make a head bow, others a profound bow, some genuflect, some make a sign of the cross, and others do nothing. But the bishops assigned the simplest of gestures, one that nearly anyone may do and that could promote uniformity at communion time: a bow of the head.

A bow of the body is made to the altar (GIRM 275b). This happens at the priest's prayers that precede his proclamation of the gospel in the absence of a deacon, and before he washes his hands. He joins others in a bow of the body at the words of the incarnation during the Creed, and he makes another bow in Eucharistic Prayer I for the part that begins, "In humble prayer." All of these bows are made in the direction of the altar, including the one during the Creed.

When a deacon asks for the blessing before the gospel, he too makes a profound bow. A minister with incense makes a profound bow to the person or object before and after the incensation (GIRM 277).

Some people perform bows that do not exist in the rubrics. For example, at the incensation, the thurifer bows to the priest or the people before and after incensing, but no rubric calls for the priest or the people to bow back. The bow shows reverence to the ones being incensed, not to the one doing the incensing.

During the preparation of the gifts, many priests bow to the server carrying the cruets or washing his hands, and they expect the server to bow back. That appears nowhere in the GIRM or the Order of Mass. When a bishop presides, he "is greeted with a deep bow by the ministers or others when they approach to assist him, when they leave after assisting him, or when they pass in front of him" (CB 76). No such rubric exists for the priest.

Even at the presentation of the gifts, no rubric calls for the exchange of bows between the ministers and the gift bearers. It would be more consistent for all of them, after the bearers have handed the gifts to the ministers, to make a profound bow to the altar (CB 72).

Sometimes the missing rubric is clearly an oversight. For example, before a solemn blessing or prayer over the people, the deacon or the priest says, "Bow down for the blessing." Oddly, the rubric that the people do as they are told is missing from both the GIRM and the Order of Mass. A too-literal reading of this omission would have them stare back standing erect in defiance. Surely, they are supposed to respond to the command, all of them making a profound bow. Such a communal profound bow would be quite moving to witness, but few congregations execute it together.

Even at the end of Mass, when the deacon or priest commands the people to go, the rubrics only describe the exit of the ministers. Obviously, the people are expected to do as the dismissal formula commands.

Catholics genuflect to the Most Blessed Sacrament, bow their heads at sacred names, and make a profound bow before other objects and persons. Consistently performing specific signs of reverence for individual purposes lends more meaning to them; so does not performing signs of reverence when none appropriately exists.

Incense

The rules for incensation are in GIRM 277. These received more detail in the 2011 Missal but have largely gone unnoticed. One therefore sees considerable variation in the practices. The present rules will surprise many priests.

When the thurifer presents the open thurible to the presider, he adds incense and makes the sign of the cross over the smoke, saying nothing. The thurifer may need instructions to wait until the presider finishes making the sign of the cross before safely closing the lid after the priest withdraws his hand.

A minister makes a profound bow to the person or object before and after incensing. An exception applies to the altar and the offerings. This is hard to remember: The presider does not bow to the altar when incensing it. The GIRM does not explain why, but it probably aims to reduce the number of bows. Both at the beginning of Mass and again after blessing God for the bread and wine, the priest has already bowed to the altar just before taking the thurible in hand. If the cross rests on the altar or near it, he incenses it first, bowing before and after. If it is elsewhere, he incenses it when he passes by. Not bowing to the altar before incensing it then avoids a duplication. However, the omission may also pertain to the symbolic relationship between the altar and the cross. Both are incensed, but the priest bows only to the cross. In doing so, he is in a sense bowing to the altar that it interprets.

How many times does the minister swing the censer? The 2011 Missal inserted these clarifications, which have largely gone unnoticed:

> Three swings of the thurible are used to incense: the Most Blessed Sacrament, a relic of the Holy Cross and images of the Lord exposed for public veneration, the offerings for the Sacrifice of the Mass, the altar cross, the *Book of the Gospels*, the paschal candle, the Priest, and the people.
>
> Two swings of the thurible are used to incense relics and images of the Saints exposed for public veneration; this should be done, however, only at the beginning of the celebration, following the incensation of the altar.
>
> The altar is incensed with single swings of the thurible. (GIRM 277)

Therefore, when the entrance procession reaches the altar, the priest receives the thurible. He does not add more incense upon reaching the sanctuary. When a bishop presides, if more incense is needed when he reaches the sanctuary, presumably after a lengthy procession of ministers, an acolyte is to add it, not the bishop himself (CB 131). The GIRM seems to assume that more incense will typically not be needed so quickly after it was inserted into the censer at the start of the procession.

If the cross is on or near the altar, the presider bows to the cross, swings the censer three times, and bows to the cross again. Then he walks around the altar without bowing as he crosses the middle, incensing it with single swings. If the cross is not on or near the altar, he incenses the altar first without bowing to it, but when he approaches the cross, wherever it is, he bows to the cross, swings the censer three times, bows to the cross a second time, and then resumes single swings around the altar.

Two different Latin expressions describe these swings: *tribus ductibus* in the case of the cross, *singulis ictibus* in the case of the altar. The Missal's English translation uses the same noun for both of them: "three swings" in the first case and "single swings" in the second. Some commentators believe that *ductibus* means "double swings." However, the words *tribus ductibus* mean "three swings," ones that go out and come back. The word *ductibus* comes from *duco*, a verb meaning lead, draw, or pull. It gives us English words such as "introduce" and "produce." The word *ictibus* comes from *ico*, meaning a strike, a stab, or a pulse. It is one source behind the English word "inflict." In the context of incensation at an altar, it probably means an up-and-down motion, rather than one that goes back and forth as before a cross. At Vatican ceremonies, the pope and other ministers do not distinguish the types of swings for the altar and other objects, and they execute double swings for anyone or anything besides the altar. However, "three swings" means "three [single] swings," each one going out and coming back one time.

At the preparation of the gifts, many priests add several circles clockwise and counterclockwise. But the Missal makes no mention of them:

> The Priest incenses the offerings with three swings of the thurible or by making the Sign of the Cross over the offerings with the thurible before going on to incense the cross and the altar. (GIRM 277)

He has a choice: either three swings toward the offerings or a cross over the offerings. That is all.

The only reference to the direction of swings is in the description of Mass with a bishop, and there only at the proclamation of the gospel, when the deacon swings the censer "in the center, to the left, and to the right" (CB 74). Although no reason is given, it seems to affirm the spread of the gospel, making this multidirectional swing appropriate even at Masses without the bishop. At other parts of the Mass, however, the rubrics seem to imply three swings in the center.

Few priests execute the incensations as described in GIRM 277. Some dismiss these concerns as pointless niceties. However, the simplification of these rules aims at consistency in practice and avoidance of excess. At Mass, there is no hierarchy of incense swings: the bishop, priests, the people, the cross, and the offerings all receive three of them. Even the newly consecrated elements receive the same reverence: three swings. The smoke equalizes the Body of Christ with the principle elements of the Mass, all sharing a fragrance that they hope will please God.

Chair, altar, ambo

The presider's chair provides more than a place to sit. It designates a place for standing. Some priests place a lectern at the chair. Especially in Masses without an altar server, such a lectern holds the Missal for the introductory rites, freeing the priest to extend his arms for the collect. Choosing a small unadorned lectern will keep it from competing with the primary furnishings, such as the ambo. Still, a lectern does not substitute for the proper training and usage of servers, whose presence exemplifies the diversity of gifts among the people of God.

Mass begins at the chair. After the priest venerates the altar, "he goes to the chair" (OM 1). Some priests remain at the altar for the beginning of Mass, but there is no provision for it. Celebrating the entire Mass at the altar overly blurs its parts; the liturgy makes important spatial distinctions. Presiding at the introductory rites from the chair, the priest preserves the altar for its proper function during the Liturgy of the Eucharist. Before Mass begins, a cloth covers the altar, and the only other items that may rest upon it are the cross, candles, and *Book of the Gospels* (GIRM 117, 306). Even these may occupy other places. The Missal is to be at the chair (GIRM 118). The GIRM is protective about the altar:

> For only what is required for the celebration of the Mass may be placed on the altar table: namely, from the beginning of the celebration until the proclamation of the Gospel, the *Book of the Gospels*; then from the Presentation of the Gifts until the purification of the vessels, the chalice with the paten, a ciborium, if nec-

> essary, and, finally, the corporal, the purificator, the pall, and the Missal. (306)

The altar is not a shelf where other items may rest: eyeglasses, hymnals, cruets, the water basin, hand sanitizer, or car keys. It is a sacred table. Although the English translation does not draw this out, at several points the GIRM refers to the *mensa*, the top of the altar, as a particularly sacred spot. After a wedding, the altar is not a table where photographers may rest their cameras. While the church is being decorated, the altar is not a bench where volunteers set vases and scissors. The top of the altar is sacred territory, twenty-four hours a day.

The ambo is used for proclaiming the readings, singing the responsorial psalm, preaching, and the universal prayer. At the Easter Vigil, it is the place for the *Exsultet*. It is not to be used at other times. "The dignity of the ambo requires that only a minister of the word should stand at it" (GIRM 309). Song leaders use another microphone. Announcements are made from that mic or from the presider's chair. Even before Mass, if someone makes an announcement, the ambo is not the proper place for it. It is for the word of God. "It is better for the commentator, cantor, or director of singing, for example, not to use the ambo."[9] Preaching takes place at the ambo, the chair or another worthy place (GIRM 136), but not at the altar.

Maintaining the sacredness of these furnishings and spaces will help everyone appreciate their purpose.

The corporal

Some priests leave the corporal resting atop the altar round the clock. Some decorators use corporals like doilies, placing them beneath flower arrangements, near statues, or on the gifts table. However, the corporal provides a specific, limited function for the Liturgy of the Eucharist.

Before Mass the corporal is kept at the credence table (GIRM 118c). It comes to the altar at the preparation of the gifts, after the universal prayer (GIRM 139). The priest places the bread and wine upon the

[9] Introduction to the *Lectionary for Mass*, 33.

corporal only after the prayers "Blessed are you, Lord God of all creation" (GIRM 141, 142). He or the deacon checks the corporal for fragments after communion (NDC[10] 51, GIRM 163). Then it is folded and removed from the altar. The corporal is the specific locus on the altar for the sacrifice of the Mass.

Traditionally, after communion, the corporal is folded in upon itself in order to contain fragments. Some ministers misunderstand this. At the preparation of the gifts, they approach the altar, corporal in hand, they open it up, suspend it, give it a shake, and place it on the altar, often upside down. However, shaking the corporal could let fly consecrated fragments remaining from its previous usage, and placing it upside down makes it more difficult to fold after communion.

Ideally the minister who carries the corporal from the credence table places it flat upon the altar and unfolds it there in its place. After communion, it is folded inwardly and carried away. Even though the priest should have checked for fragments before this, it would be prudent to open it again in the sacristy over the *sacrarium* and there give it shake.

The corporal seems like an unimportant piece of cloth, but it is the place that receives the offerings of the people, where the Holy Spirit transforms the bread and wine into the Body and Blood of Christ, and from which the faithful are fed.

Raising the elements

At different moments of the Mass, both before and after the consecration of the bread and wine, the priest takes these elements in hand. The rubrics designate different heights for these moments. When properly observed, they show the significance of these actions, especially those within the eucharistic prayer.

At the preparation of the gifts, the priest "takes the paten with the bread and holds it slightly raised above the altar with both hands" (OM 23) Then he prays, "Blessed are you, Lord God of all creation." Similarly, he "then takes the chalice and holds it slightly raised above

[10] Norms for the Distribution and Reception of Holy Communion under Both Kinds in the United States of America.

the altar with both hands" and prays, "Blessed are you, Lord God of all creation" (OM 25).

These rubrics are new to the postconciliar Mass. They suggest that the action is moving downwards. The priest has received the gifts from the people or the server, and before placing them on the corporal, while praising God, he suspends them a moment, "slightly raised above the altar." Some priests hold them high, thinking that the words addressed to God call for a raised gesture. It does not. This gesture settles the gifts for their purpose. The priest says the words while he pauses the grand action of moving the gifts on their way down to the altar's *mensa*.

Later, to begin the institution narrative and consecration, the priest "takes the bread and, holding it slightly raised above the altar," pronounces the words (OM 89). A few moments after that, "he takes the chalice and, holding it slightly raised above the altar, continues" (OM 90).

The height for holding the bread and wine at the words of consecration is the same as for the preparation of the gifts: "slightly raised." Most priests do hold the elements low at this point, especially because the rubrics instruct him to make a slight bow while reciting these sacred words. A presider is to hold the bread and wine at the preparation of the gifts in the same way.

The Order of Mass next instructs the priest about the gesture that follows each part of the consecration. After pronouncing the words over the bread, "he shows the consecrated host to the people." Similarly, after the consecration of the wine, "he shows the chalice to the people" (OM 89, 90).

The rubric does not require him to use "both hands" as it does when he receives the gifts, but showing the host and chalice with only one hand may look informal or even careless to the people who are meant to adore it.

The verb here, "shows," has not changed: It is the same verb used in the preconciliar Mass. When the priest prayed the canon facing the apse, however, there was only one way he could "show" the people behind him the host and the chalice. He had to raise it high above his head. Now that he faces the people, the gesture need not be so high. He can show it by moving his arms forward more than up.

The rubric in the Order of Mass does not say that the priest "elevates" the host. He is not raising the host to God; he is showing it to the people for their adoration. Often the English translation of the GIRM mistakenly calls this part of the Mass the "elevation."[11] The Latin word in each case is *ostensionem*, or "showing," not *elevationem*, in perfect harmony with the words in the Order of Mass. The GIRM in Latin speaks of "elevation" only in reference to the *Book of the Gospels* (GIRM 120, 133, 194), which is carried slightly elevated in procession; to the priest's action at the close of the eucharistic prayer (GIRM 180); and to the height of a sanctuary (GIRM 295).

The proper "elevation" according to the Order of Mass comes at the end of the eucharistic prayer, as GIRM 180 concurs. Before the doxology, the priest "takes the chalice and the paten with the host and, raising both, he says: Through him. . . ." (OM 98). This is the only place where the Order of Mass speaks of "raising" the elements, and in Latin, the verb is indeed *elevans*. The preconciliar Missal modified the same verb at this point with the Latin word *parum* ("a little bit"). The revised Order of Mass struck the word *parum* after the council. Clearly, the object was to have the priest raise the host and the chalice highest at the conclusion of the eucharistic prayer. This coincides with the people's amen. As the priest brings the prayer of thanksgiving and consecration to a close, he makes an elevation, his highest gesture up, as if summarizing all that the prayer has said.

At communion, the priest genuflects, "takes the host and, holding it slightly raised above the paten or above the chalice," says "Behold the Lamb of God" (OM 132). Again, the host is "slightly raised," but this time over the paten or the chalice. Many priests lift the chalice as well, but the rubric never instructs him to do so. In the preconciliar Mass he turned to face the people at this point, so he had to hold the chalice to avoid suspending the host over air and threatening problems should it fall. Today, while facing the people, he may hold the host over the paten or chalice resting on the altar. He then consumes the host. However, he pauses the motion of bringing the host from the altar to his mouth long enough to pray, "Lord, I am not worthy." The height of the host here is only slightly raised, as if the presider is in the process of receiving communion.

[11] GIRM 150, 179, 222c, 227c, 230c, 233c, 274, 276.

When the priest gives communion to the people, he "raises a host slightly and shows it to each of the communicants, saying: The Body of Christ" (OM 134). This instruction combines two of the preceding verbs: raising the host slightly and showing it to the communicant. The word "show" is identical to the one in the consecration. If the priest models his gesture at the consecration after his gesture for giving communion, he will probably be closer to what the rubrics intend.

To review, the bread and wine are slightly raised at the preparation of the gifts on their way down to the altar, during the words of consecration, and before the priest receives his communion. The elements are shown to the people at the consecration and to each communicant at communion. The priest elevates the elements highest at the end of the eucharistic prayer. A review of these heights will help the people interpret the parts of the Mass, including the proper flow of the entire eucharistic prayer. It will even help them link their own communion to the consecration of the bread and wine.

These small rubrical points conceal larger beliefs. The Order of Mass and the GIRM consistently present a eucharistic theology emerging from the arc of the entire Mass. They offer reverence to the Blessed Sacrament, while viewing the entire eucharistic prayer as a single piece, a complete prayer of thanksgiving and offering to God.

7

Concelebration: The State of the Question

The Catholic Church invites priests to concelebrate for special events when disparate priests gather, and on ordinary occasions where priests live in common. In the latter case, communities generally prefer a common celebration of the Eucharist to multiple smaller celebrations—even private Masses—on the same day.

The very sight of concelebrating priests impresses many Catholics, who are much aware of the clergy shortage and of how busy priests can be. At a funeral, for example, some Catholics conclude that the presence of concelebrants measures the impact that the deceased person had on the life of the church beyond family, friends, and coworkers.

Concelebration appropriately expresses "the unity of the Priesthood, of the Sacrifice, and also of the whole People of God" (GIRM 199). The gathering of vested priests shows them exercising their role together. Their mutual participation emphasizes the unity of the sacrifice in which they communally participate. By assuming their role and having others fulfill theirs, "the sacred ministers and the faithful [take] part in [the Mass], according to the state proper to each" (GIRM 17). The bishop regulates the discipline of concelebration (GIRM 202, 387).

The word applies to the participation of priests. The Vatican has warned against calling Mass a concelebration "in the univocal sense, of the Priest along with the people who are present."[1] An earlier usage of the word applies to the way that the heavenly court celebrates together with the earthly church. Five prefaces use the Latin word for "concelebrate" in this way: Lent IV, Blessed Virgin Mary I, Common II, St. Joseph, and the Exaltation of the Holy Cross. The oldest of these, the one for Mary, comes from the Gelasian Sacramentary around the seventh century. However, the Missal's English translation speaks of these two worlds "worshiping together;" in Latin they "concelebrate."

A priest may always choose concelebration instead of presiding, unless the welfare of the people suggests otherwise (canon 902). For example, to facilitate the participation of the faithful at Sunday Mass, two priests living in the same parish rectory each preside at separate liturgies, rather than concelebrate at a single one.

The Missal explicitly prescribes concelebration for certain ceremonies: the ordination of bishops and priests, the blessing of an abbot, and the chrism Mass. It also recommends concelebration at Holy Thursday's Mass of the Lord's Supper and the Easter Vigil, (the days on which priests are not allowed to celebrate individually,) and for other gatherings of priests, both with and without the bishop (GIRM 199).

Nonetheless, when the bishop is present, "it is most fitting that he himself celebrate the Eucharist and associate Priests with himself in the sacred action as concelebrants" (GIRM 92). Concelebration with the bishop is "to be held in particularly high regard" (GIRM 203). This especially pertains to solemn days of the liturgical year, the ordination of a bishop, the chrism Mass and other occasions. On any day that priests gather with their bishop, the Missal recommends concelebration, referencing *Eucharisticum Mysterium* 47: "In these cases the sign of the unity of the Priesthood and also of the Church inherent in every concelebration is made more clearly manifest" (GIRM 203).

[1] Congregation for Divine Worship and the Discipline of the Sacraments, *Redemptionis Sacramentum* [RS]*: On Certain Matters to Be Observed or to Be Avoided regarding the Most Holy Eucharist* (Vatican City, 2004), 42, citing the 1947 encyclical of Pius XII *Mediator Dei*, 83, long before the post–Vatican II practice of concelebration.

For religious communities, the Missal especially encourages concelebration at the conventual Mass, where "all should exercise their function according to the Order or ministry they have received" (GIRM 114).

In spite of the church's preference, some priests decline the opportunities to concelebrate.[2] Some celebrate individually, presumably because they find the solitary celebration more spiritually enriching that a concelebrated one. Canon law stresses that he is to have at least some member of the faithful participating, except for a just and reasonable cause (canon 906). The Roman Missal includes an Order of Mass with the participation of a single minister. It does not provide an order of service for Mass without one, though "In this case, the greetings, the instructions, and the blessing at the end of Mass are omitted" (GIRM 254). The greetings are the occasions when the priest says, "The Lord be with you," or its equivalents in the introductory rites. The instructions are the commentaries he may give at times such as after the greeting in the introductory rites or the announcements at the end (GIRM 31). Otherwise, he recites all the parts of the Mass himself, including, "Pray, brothers and sisters." Presiding alone almost seems awkward by design because the nature of the Mass cries out for at least one other person to be present. Nonetheless, some priests choose this even when concelebration is an option. After all, canon law earnestly recommends that priests celebrate Mass daily (canon 904).

Some decline to concelebrate because they preside at another Mass the same day. Canon law restricts a priest to one Mass a day except in cases where the law permits more (canon 905 §1); this probably means occasions listed in the Missal, such as the day of the chrism Mass, Easter, Christmas, and All Souls Day (GIRM 204). However, the Missal names one more permission for circumstances when the bishop presides: "a Priest who concelebrates with the Bishop . . . on the occasion of a gathering of Priests, may celebrate Mass again for the benefit of the faithful" (GIRM 204e). Hence, a priest who presides at one Mass has the faculty to concelebrate another Mass with the

[2] For a fine presentation of the situation within the religious communities of Jesuits, see "Jesuits and Eucharistic Concelebration" by James J. Conn, and "Jesuits, the Ministerial Priesthood, and Eucharistic Concelebration" by John F. Baldovin, in *Studies in the Spirituality of Jesuits* 51/1 (Spring 2019).

bishop the same day. In practice, many priests celebrate three or four Masses on some days due to the needs of the people.

Some priests attend a concelebrated Mass in choir dress. The Missal permits it, but does not recommend it (GIRM 114). It recalls the oft-repeated principle that all present perform the functions that fit their state.[3] "It is preferable that Priests who are present at a celebration of the Eucharist, unless excused for a just reason, should usually exercise the function proper to their Order and hence take part as concelebrants, wearing sacred vestments. Otherwise, they wear their proper choir dress or a surplice over a cassock." Nonetheless, the Missal calls for seats to be arranged for such non-concelebrating priests (GIRM 310). Although the GIRM gives no further instructions for them, they logically assume the postures appropriate to the laity who participate at Mass, not making the gestures that concelebrants make, and receiving communion as the laity, rather than as concelebrants. Some priests in choir who are celebrating another Mass that day may decline communion, but canon law permits communion at a second celebration on the same day (canon 917).

Still other priests prefer neither to concelebrate nor to wear choir dress, but to take a place among the faithful at Mass. Some priests make this choice out of solidarity with those who hold that viewing many concelebrants clericalizes the liturgy and marginalizes the leadership potential of women. The CDWDS offered the strongest objection to the practice: "It is not fitting, except in rare and exceptional cases and with reasonable cause, for [priests] to participate at Mass, as regards to externals, in the manner of the lay faithful" (RS 128).

Some visiting priests do not concelebrate because they have not secured the required letter of suitability from their own superior and permission from the host diocese. Canon law permits a priest to celebrate if he presents a letter of introduction from his ordinary, or if prudent judgment sees no reason to impede his participation (canon 903). The Missal says that visiting priests should be "gladly admitted" if their standing has been ascertained (GIRM 200). The CDWDS says that either a *celebret* less than one year old or a prudent judgment should suffice; "Let the Bishops take measures to put a stop to any contrary practice" (RS 111). The scandals concerning clerical abuse

[3] GIRM 17; SC 28; *Lumen Gentium*, 11; RS 128.

have cemented stricter requirements in place, however, and priests may not be able to concelebrate without adequate documentation.

Priests who do not know the language of the celebration and cannot pronounce the required parts of the eucharistic prayer, according to the CDWDS, "should not concelebrate, but instead should attend the celebration in choral dress in accordance with the norms" (RS 113).

Occasionally, a priest does not concelebrate simply because he shows up for Mass late. The Missal says, "No one is ever to join a concelebration or to be admitted as a concelebrant once the Mass has already begun" (GIRM 206).

Canon law forbids priests to concelebrate with ministers of churches or ecclesial communities who do not enjoy full communion with the Catholic Church.[4]

Mass stipends have had an impact on concelebrations. Canon law permits any priest celebrating or concelebrating Mass to receive an offering to apply the Mass for a specific intention (canon 945 §1). However, a priest who concelebrates a second Mass on the same day cannot accept an offering for it (canon 951 §2). In a religious community housed together, some priests may prefer not to concelebrate at a Mass when no laypeople are in attendance, but they may elect to do so in order to satisfy a stipend.

Apparently to honor the stipend, the parts of the Mass concelebrants speak aloud come from the eucharistic prayer: the epiclesis, institution narrative and consecration, the anamnesis and offering. Concelebrants do not recite aloud the entire eucharistic prayer, but only the central part. Nor do they recite in common any other presidential prayer. History shows times that concelebrants did not even recite the words of the eucharistic prayer but concerns about stipends probably contributed to a change.

[4] Canon 908. See also RS 172c, which adds ministers of communities that have no apostolic succession or do not acknowledge the sacramentality of orders.

8

Concelebration: History

Concelebration has appeared in some manner throughout all of church history.[1] Even the New Testament offers some provocative passages. Paul reminded Timothy of the gift he received through the prophetic word with the imposition of hands of not one presbyter, but of the presbyterate (1 Tim 4:14). Paul described participation in the Blood and Body of Christ through the cup of blessing that "we" bless and the bread that "we" break (1 Cor 10:16). James wrote that those who were sick should summon the presbyters of the church because "they" should pray over and anoint the sick (Jas 5:14).

If the treatise *Apostolic Tradition* can be dated to the fourth century, it provides a tantalizing early piece of evidence. During the celebration for the ordination of a bishop, just before the eucharistic prayer, the deacon brought him the offerings, and the bishop laid his hands on them, as did the presbyters,[2] who apparently were concelebrating. The bishop alone spoke the words of the eucharistic prayer, however. Indeed, he could improvise these, making it nearly impossible for

[1] For greater detail, see the work of Markus Tymister, *La concelebrazione eucarística: Storia. Questioni teologiche. Rito*, 2nd ed., revised and corrected (Rome: CLV Edizioni Liturgiche, 2018).

[2] Paul Bradshaw, Maxwell E. Johnson, and L. Edward Phillips, *The Apostolic Tradition: A Commentary*, ed. Harold W. Attridge (Minneapolis: Augsburg Fortress, 2002), p. 8.

anyone to pray aloud with him. The presbyters thus participated by this gesture only, not by words. Their action happened before the eucharistic prayer begins, but it seems to be their way of concelebrating with the presiding bishop.

Similar evidence arises in the contemporaneous *Mystagogical Catecheses* of Cyril of Jerusalem (+386), where he instructed the newly baptized about the Eucharist. Explaining the parts of the liturgy, he began with the washing of hands that preceded the eucharistic prayer:

> You saw the deacon offering water for washing to the [bishop] and to the presbyters encircling God's altar. Of course, he did not do this because their bodies were dirty. . . . So there is no doubt that the washing of the hands represents symbolically freedom from sins.[3]

Here, the presbyters encircled the altar together with the bishop. The deacon washed the hands of all of them for ritual purity, not physical cleanliness. Although the bishop alone recited the eucharistic prayer, this action suggests the understanding that the presbyters "concelebrated" with him.

By the beginning of the seventh century, the Roman Canon had reached its developed form under Pope Gregory the Great (+604), which thus permitted a more uniform recitation of the eucharistic prayer throughout the Roman Rite.[4] At certain papal celebrations, the bishops, archdeacons, and deacons arranged themselves in hierarchical order for the offertory. After the *Sanctus*, the pope alone continued with the canon while everyone else bowed.[5]

A Roman order of service also from the seventh century shows that on four days—Easter, Pentecost, the Feast of St. Peter, and Christmas—the cardinal priests gathered with the pope, each holding a corporal into which the deacon placed three offerings, probably small loaves of bread. "All say the canon with him," holding the offerings in their hands, not on the altar, where the pope alone made the sign

[3] Edward Yarnold, *The Awe-Inspiring Rites of Initiation: The Origins of the RCIA*, 2nd ed. (Collegeville, MN: Liturgical Press, 1994), p. 90.

[4] Tymister, *La concelebrazione eucarística*, p. 70.

[5] Ordo Romanus I:86–88. Michel Andrieu, *Les Ordines Romani du Haut Moyen Age* II: Les Textes (Louvain: Spicilegium Sacrum Lovaniense, 1971), pp. 95–96.

of the cross over the offerings placed there.[6] This is the earliest testimony of a communal recitation of any eucharistic prayer, though only on specific days.

Amalarius (+850) provided similar testimony for the observance of Holy Thursday's Mass of the Lord's Supper: "The custom of the Roman Church is that in carrying out the sacrifice of Christ, the presbyters are present and carry it out together with the pope with words and hands."[7] Reciting the words out loud in common appeared at the same time as the development of the theology of the consecratory power of priests.[8]

By the twelfth century in Rome, at the consecration of a new bishop, following the Creed of the Mass, he "approaches the altar and finishes the Mass together with the one" who consecrated him.[9] More details emerged by the thirteenth century: The pope and the newly consecrated bishop, both properly vested for Mass, stood at the altar, each using his own Missal. The pope "continues according to custom and lifts his voice to recite the preface, and the newly consecrated bishop pronounces the same words more quietly and reads the rest, and he performs the things that follow in the rest of the canon of the Mass up to communion."[10]

According to Durandus, also in the thirteenth century, newly ordained priests held copies of the Missal and recited the prayers of the canon together with the bishop who presided at their ordination Mass.[11]

By this time, theologians had determined that the moment of consecration came when the priest pronounced the words of Christ at the Last Supper, "This is my body. . . . This is my blood." This posed a practical dilemma: What if a concelebrating priest reached those

[6] Ordo Romanus III:1. Andrieu, p. 131. Cf. Tymister, pp. 70–71.

[7] Amalarius, *De ecclesiastici offices libri quattro* I, 12, ed. J. P. Migne, Paris, 1864 (PL 105), col. 1016C, cited in Tymister, p. 78.

[8] Tymister, p. 82.

[9] Michel Andrieu, *Le Pontifical Romain au moyen-âge*, I: *Le Pontifical Romain du XIIe siècle* (Vatican City: Biblioteca Apostolica Vaticana, 1938), X:32, p. 151.

[10] Michel Andrieu, *Le Pontifical Romain au moyen-âge*, II: *Le Pontifical de la Curie Romaine au XIIIe siècle* (Vatican City: Biblioteca Apostolica Vaticana, 1940), XI:34, p. 365.

[11] Michel Andrieu, *Le Pontifrical Romain au moye-âge*, III: *Le Pontifical de Guillaume Durand* (Vatican City: Biblioteca Apostolica Vaticana, 1940), XIII:20, pp. 370–71.

words ahead of the bishop? Who consecrated? Lothario di Segni, the future Pope Innocent III (+1216), proposed at the end of the twelfth century that the consecration still happened simultaneously because all the clergy held the same intention.[12] Because concelebration continued at ordinations, Thomas Aquinas (+1274) took up the same question, reaching a similar resolution. He relied on Innocent III and the biblical evidence that the apostles shared communion at the Last Supper.[13] Albert the Great (+1280), however, knew a custom where the newly ordained priests made the gestures during the canon, but did not recite the words.[14] Hence, the practice, which continued for centuries at ordinations of bishops and priests, was not uniform.

In 1755, Pope Benedict XIV (+1758) issued the magisterium's first statement on concelebration, in which he acknowledged the long tradition in the Eastern Rites, while accepting the practice of priests reciting the canon together at ordination masses.[15] The 1917 Code of Canon Law forbade concelebration apart from the ordination Masses of bishops and priests as indicated in the Roman Pontifical (canon 803). However, when bishops of the Eastern Catholic Churches concelebrated a Eucharist in Rome in 1922, anticipating the 1600th anniversary of the Council of Nicaea, the sight impressed Roman Catholics and reopened the discussion.[16] The Holy Office received a question in 1957 if a priest could validly concelebrate without saying aloud the words of consecration, and it replied no.[17] Subsequently, the Roman Pontifical of 1961–1962 on the eve of the Second Vatican Council reaffirmed the longstanding practice at ordination Masses that the newly ordained priests recited the words of the consecration together with the bishop.[18]

When Vatican II convened, the topic became part of the preparatory discussion for the Constitution on the Sacred Liturgy. Concelebration entered the 1963 constitution in paragraphs 57 and 58. The council extended permission for concelebration, "which is an ap-

[12] Tymister, pp. 94–95.
[13] Tymister, pp. 104–11.
[14] Tymister, pp. 112–17.
[15] Tymister, pp. 120–23.
[16] Tymister, p. 37.
[17] Tymister, p. 187.
[18] Tymister, p. 149.

propriate way of manifesting the unity of the priesthood" (SC 57). Permissions included the chrism Mass; the Evening Mass of the Lord's Supper; Masses during councils, bishops' conferences, and synods; the blessing of an abbot; and at other Masses where priests gathered, with the permission of the ordinary. The 1983 Code of Canon Law opened the permissions more broadly: "Unless the welfare of the Christian faithful requires or suggests otherwise, priests can concelebrate the Eucharist" (canon 902).

The Sacred Congregation of Rites (Consilium) issued its *Rite of Concelebration* on March 7, 1965, even before Vatican II had concluded its work.[19] It asked concelebrants not to stand between the altar and the people in order to preserve the faithful's clear view of the rite (4), and not to join the concelebration if Mass had already begun (8). It gave instructions concerning vestments (12) and the communal recitation of the words, especially the words of consecration (13). It instructed concelebrants to gesture only when speaking aloud and to pray silently otherwise (14). In principle, not all priests do what one priest (the presider) does, just as not all lay people do what one lay person does (such as the reader), yet all participate.

The same congregation issued similar comments on concelebration in 1967 with its instruction *Eucharisticum Mysterium*.[20] It defended concelebration as a sign of the unity of the sacrifice and the priesthood, especially when the faithful are present and particularly if the bishop presides. It also expanded permissions to seminary faculties and other groups where priests gather.

Specific norms entered the GIRM from the first edition of the postconciliar Missal, and these were revised for the third edition, translated into English in 2011.

[19] Sacred Congregation of Rites (Consilium), *Rite of Concelebration*, Introduction, March 7, 1965 (Vatican Polyglot Press, 1965), 13–18. See ICEL, *Documents on the Liturgy, 1963–1979: Conciliar, Papal, and Curial Texts* (Collegeville, MN: Liturgical Press, 1982), 1794–1810.

[20] Sacred Congregation of Rites, *Eucharisticum Mysterium*, On Worship of the Eucharist (May 25, 1967), *Acta Apostolicæ Sedis* 59 (1967): 539–73; *Notitiae* 3 (1967): 225–60; ICEL, *Documents on the Liturgy*, 1276.

9

Ars Concelebrandi

As the celebration of Mass invites an *ars celebrandi*, so concelebration invites an *ars concelebrandi*. Each priest still practices intentionality, along with full, conscious, active participation, even when he concelebrates. When he does less, he neglects his duty to enter the spirit of the celebration and threatens to distract his fellow priests as well as the people in the congregation.

Self-Preparation

A concelebrant must arrive on time; he is not to be admitted if the celebration has already begun (GIRM 206). He surely may be admitted to the congregation among the laity, but not as a vested concelebrant. Although the rubrics do not comment about the end of the Mass in the same way, it would be at least courteous and at best a fulfillment of his duties for the concelebrant not to leave early either.

He vests as he does when celebrating Mass individually (GIRM 209); that is, with alb, stole, and chasuble, only the amice and cincture remaining optional (GIRM 119, 337). Alternatively, a priest may concelebrate wearing alb and stole, but the circumstance for this is a large number of concelebrants or lack of vestments (GIRM 209). White chasubles are always permitted to concelebrants and seem preferable to no chasuble (RS 124). Informality is not a reason for leaving an available chasuble on a sacristy hanger.

Whenever priests gather, happy reunions ensue. They reconnect with friends, tell stories, inquire about ministry, and learn about joys and sorrows. The conversation can be strong and loud, reminiscent of seminary days. If they gather near the communal sacred space, priests sometimes cause a distraction for the people gathering prayerfully in the nave, or they may drown out the musicians offering preludes or rehearsing the assembled faithful. The very pastors who object to people talking loudly in their parish churches are sometimes guilty of the same behavior when gathering at the cathedral or another sacred place. Lively conversation fosters priestly fraternity, but for the sake of the liturgy, the nave deserves a reverent silence.

During the course of the Mass, similar concerns arise. Priests seated near friends and colleagues naturally want to chat. Sometimes they openly critique the liturgy as it unfolds. Often their conversation causes a visible distraction for participants striving to pray, including other priests nearby. Intentionality applies to concelebrants at every moment of the liturgy. Every song, dialogue, and silence involves the full, conscious, active participation of each concelebrant.

Some concelebrants greet the lay people they recognize from present or former ministry. Before Mass begins or after its conclusion, such salutations can beautifully build up the Body of Christ. But once the liturgy has begun, and until it is completely over, a concelebrant's attention best focuses on the words and actions of the Mass. Some priests wave at someone they recognize while they are walking in procession, as if they were celebrities on parade before an admiring crowd. They need the reminder, "This is not about you." It is about Christ. At all times, the liturgy is about Christ, and he deserves a priest's rapt attention.

Sacristan Notes

A sacristan prepares space for concelebrants. Judging the appropriate amount of seating proves challenging at events where the number of concelebrants is unknown until they arrive (GIRM 207, 294, 310). A sacristan makes available copies of texts such as the eucharistic prayer if these are needed (GIRM 207). Similarly, if some priests vest in choir dress, they also need designated seating (GIRM 310; CB 123).

A sufficient number of chalices and quantity of wine is readied (GIRM 207; NDC 31). These measurements can often be adjusted after the Mass begins when the sacristan sees the precise number of concelebrants, remembering that priests in choir dress may also receive communion under both kinds (GIRM 283; NDC 23). If concelebrants are to receive communion by intinction, the sacristan may prepare a smaller quantity of wine.

Concelebrants as Deacons or Lay Ministers

Ordinarily, each minister fulfills the role appointed. However, at times there is no deacon, but there are concelebrants. At other times, there are no lay ministers, but there are concelebrants. In these instances, a concelebrant may serve those roles.

The Missal says rather strongly that without a deacon, his functions "are to be carried out by some of the concelebrants." It encourages the use of "suitable faithful laypeople," but if there are none, their roles too "are carried out" by concelebrants (GIRM 208). The Missal does not just permit concelebrants to fulfill these roles; it expects that they will.

This is not always observed, especially in the absence of deacons. Frequently concelebrants do just what concelebrants do, and the presider absorbs the role of the deacon. At other times when suitable lay ministers are present, they may presume that a concelebrant should function as a reader, for example; but the Missal discourages the practice (GIRM 208).

When a bishop presides, three deacons preferably serve: one to proclaim the gospel and minister at the altar, and two others to assist the bishop. (In practice, only two deacons often serve, one assuming responsibilities for the Liturgy of the Word, and the other for the Liturgy of the Eucharist, while a master of ceremonies assists the bishop; however, the GIRM and CB never envision such an arrangement.) Whether the local custom is for three or two deacons to assist the bishop, if there are no deacons, "their ministries should be carried out by presbyters, who, vested as priests, concelebrate with the bishop (CB 122)." A priest who performs the role of a deacon wears the priestly stole and chasuble, not the diaconal stole and dalmatic.

Without a deacon present, his duties fall sometimes to a lay minister, and sometimes to a concelebrant. A layperson could list the invocations in the third form of the penitential act, read the petitions of the universal prayer and assist with incensing. However, a concelebrant could introduce the Mass, could list the invocations in the third form of the penitential act, would read the gospel, assist at the altar with the chalice, invite the sign of peace, and give the dismissal. In the first instance, a layperson may perform those diaconal functions that a priest need not or should not do; in the second instance a priest performs functions proper to a deacon's ordained ministry. Hence, at times a deacon's absence calls for more involvement from the laity; at other times it calls for more involvement from priests.

The Introductory Rites

For the entrance procession, concelebrating priests walk ahead of the principal celebrant (GIRM 210). When a bishop presides, the processional details are clear; they also logically apply when a priest presides with concelebrants. The processional order goes as follows: server with incense, servers with cross and candles, non-concelebrating clergy in choir dress, the deacon with the *Book of the Gospels*, other deacons walking two by two, concelebrants walking two by two, the bishop, the two deacons who assist him, other servers who assist with his miter and pastoral staff (CB 128). Even on occasions without a bishop but with multiple deacons and priests, the deacons precede the concelebrants in procession.

If the procession to the altar passes a chapel with the Blessed Sacrament reserved, the ministers neither stop nor genuflect to the tabernacle (CB 71, 128). Upon first entering the church, however, it is fitting for all, even priests, to adore the Blessed Sacrament with a visit or at least a genuflection (CB 71). Although the rubrics do not explain why there is no genuflection during a procession, they probably presume that each minister made a proper reverence upon entering the church, and that stops and genuflections would inhibit the smooth flow of the procession.

If the people are singing an entrance song (GIRM 48), the music logically includes the priests. Concelebrants process best when they take part in the opening chant, singing the words and absorbing their meaning. Concentrating on the text will help priests avoid the temptation to wave at people in the pews, who should also be attentively singing the words.

Upon arriving at the sanctuary, the concelebrants make appropriate signs of reverence. Ministers genuflect only if the tabernacle with the Blessed Sacrament is situated in the sanctuary (GIRM 274). The guidelines for concelebrants never mention this, though they omit the genuflection for ministers passing a tabernacle in procession. Consequently, where the tabernacle is in the sanctuary, two opinions prevail: that GIRM 274 applies to concelebrants, meaning that they should genuflect to the tabernacle before reverencing the altar with a bow and a kiss; or that the omission of this reverence in passages such as GIRM 211 and CB 130 implies that concelebrants reverence only the altar with a bow and a kiss, and not the tabernacle with a genuflection.

In practice, where the tabernacle is in the sanctuary, few priests use all three reverences even when they preside without concelebrants: a genuflection to the tabernacle, a bow to the altar, and a kiss to the altar. Many priests genuflect, omit the bow to the altar, and then kiss the altar.

With concelebrants, in view of the value of avoiding stops and genuflections that slow down the procession, it seems more likely that the rubrics intend for concelebrants not to genuflect even when the tabernacle is in the sanctuary; rather, they make a profound bow to the altar and then kiss the altar.

After reverencing the altar, concelebrants take the places prepared for them before the Mass. When a bishop presides, if there are no deacons, two concelebrants stand near the bishop's chair, ready to assist him (CB 131).

An introduction to the Mass may be given after the sign of the cross and the greeting. At Mass with the bishop, if he does not give this, a deacon or concelebrant may do so (CB 132). Especially if the pastor of the parish is concelebrating with the bishop, it may be courteous for the pastor to assume this role, extending the parish's welcome to the bishop.

For the penitential act, the presider may lead it. If the third form is used, however, a deacon or concelebrant may offer the three invocations. In fact, a lay minister may offer them (CB 132).

The priest, cantor, or choir begins the Gloria (GIRM 53). When a bishop presides, a concelebrant may intone it (CB 135). The rubric does not explain why a concelebrant may take this role at a pontifical

Mass, but it could be a question of musical gifts, or the recognition that starting the Gloria is not exclusively the role of the presider.

The Liturgy of the Word

Concelebrants stay in their places for the liturgy of the word (GIRM 212). This politely reminds them not to usurp the role of a suitable lay minister proclaiming the readings, or even of a deacon proclaiming the gospel. Concelebrants assume the postures of the principal celebrant.

When there is no deacon, a concelebrant proclaims the gospel. If the bishop presides, this concelebrant requests the blessing from the bishop; if a priest presides, a concelebrant does not request this blessing from him; instead, he prepares himself as if he were the presider of a Mass without a deacon, reciting the appropriate formula (GIRM 212). The GIRM does not explain this, but the practice suggests that in a Mass without bishop or deacon, a concelebrant proclaims the gospel as one among peers, not as one delegated by the bishop.[1]

At the conclusion of the gospel, the deacon takes the book to the bishop, who kisses it; or the deacon himself may kiss the book at the ambo reciting the appropriate formula. If a concelebrant proclaims the gospel in the absence of a deacon at a Mass when the bishop presides, he has the same options: He may carry the book to the bishop or perform the reverence himself (CB 141). The *Book of the Gospels* is closed when in processions at the start of Mass or from the altar to the ambo. As is the practice at the Vatican, the priest or concelebrant who carries the book to the bishop logically keeps it closed, and the bishop kisses the closed book, not the proclaimed passage.

The presider usually gives the homily, but a concelebrant may do so (GIRM 213). In fact, even a non-concelebrating bishop or priest may preach the homily (GIRM 66, RS 64).

The presider introduces the prayer of the faithful, and a deacon or lay minister leads the petitions (GIRM 71). Even at Mass with the bishop, the ministers who may list the petitions are a deacon, cantor, reader, or some other person (CB 144), but not the presider nor explicitly a concelebrant. In the absence of a deacon, then, a suitable lay minister performs this function—unless none is there.

[1] Tymister, *La concelebrazione eucarística*, p. 279.

Preparation of the Gifts

As with the Liturgy of the Word, at the preparation of the gifts the Missal calls for the concelebrants to stay in their places (GIRM 214, CB 145). Even so, in the absence of a deacon, one of the concelebrants could fulfill his role, assisting in the reception of the gifts and preparing the chalice by adding water to the wine.

If incense is used, the deacon or server incenses the concelebrants after the presider. The separate incensation of concelebrants explicitly appears in the rubrics only in the case of a bishop presiding (CB 149), but it may pertain to other celebrations when a priest presides. A thurifer customarily incenses concelebrating bishops before concelebrating priests, but no rubric calls for it.

Usually a deacon assists with this incensation, but in his absence a lay server performs this function. It need not be a concelebrant, who rather is among those being incensed.

Before the washing of the hands, a deacon may remove the ring from the bishop who presides (CB 150). In the absence of a deacon, a concelebrant could assist because the rubric does not assign the task to anyone else. Of course, a bishop may remove his own ring without assistance, or leave it on.

The Eucharistic Prayer

Concelebrants approach the altar after the prayer over the offerings. They stand around it without obstructing the rites at the altar and the view of the faithful (GIRM 215, CB 153). In some settings, the sanctuary cannot accommodate a large number of concelebrants, so they remain at their places. If they do move closer to the altar, a thoughtful presider will wait until all are in place, following the principle of doing one thing at a time. A pause allows the other priests to concentrate first on taking their positions and then on their prayer, and it prevents distracting the people from the dialogue and the preface.

In stationing themselves, concelebrants may consider the gestures they will soon make. If there is room, they may give themselves ample space to extend their arms as wide as they choose. The rubrics do not say how wide a priest should extend his hands while he prays; some priests choose a narrow distance, while others go further. When concelebrants are many and the space is constricted, however, even those who prefer a wider extension may be restricted by the proximity of the next concelebrant.

Some priests may need a copy of the eucharistic prayer, especially, but not exclusively, those who are newly ordained or who are praying in a language not of their birth. Holding a booklet will limit their ability to make gestures. Because historical evidence shows multiple Missals in use at a concelebration, because the presider's Missal commonly rests on the altar, and out of practicality, concelebrants near the altar could set copies of the eucharistic prayer there. Ideally, concelebrants have sufficiently memorized their parts that copies are not needed when they recite in common.

The deacon takes a place near the altar, but "behind" the concelebrants standing around the presider (GIRM 215, CB 153). When the bishop presides, no one stands between him and the concelebrants or between the concelebrants and the altar (CB 153). This visually distinguishes the role of the priests from that of the deacons, a master of ceremonies, or a server. In a large group of concelebrants, the deacon logically stands behind only the few who may be stationed next to the presider, not behind every concelebrant in the room.

Before the eucharistic prayer begins, when a bishop presides, a deacon removes the bishop's skullcap and hands it to a minister (CB 153). In the absence of a deacon, a concelebrant may do that. No provision is made for a server or master of ceremonies to remove the bishop's skullcap; the deacon's action seems related to his role before the Mass begins when he places the miter on the bishop's head, and the pallium around the shoulders of an archbishop (CB 126). In practice, some bishops remove their own skullcap. The skullcap does not remain on the altar but is carried away. This preserves the function of the altar of sacrifice and the correct usage of a side table.

Throughout the eucharistic prayer, a deacon stands near in order to assist with the chalice and the Missal. He may uncover and recover the ciborium; he may place the pall over and aside from the chalice; he may turn the pages of the Missal (GIRM 215, CB 153, 155). In the absence of a deacon, a concelebrant may assist the presider in these duties. The use of such covers is optional: The vessels are uncovered only if they have been covered (CB 155). The rubrics do not address the covering of multiple chalices that may be resting on the altar; the covering of one surely suffices, and even that is not required.

The principal celebrant alone leads the preface dialogue and the preface. All concelebrants join the people in the *Sanctus* (GIRM 216). Afterwards, from the *Sanctus* to the epiclesis, only the presider or the individual concelebrant who speaks extends his hands as he prays (GIRM 219–21, 226, 229, 232).

If sound amplification is required, individual concelebrants may speak into the microphone on the altar or one that they are wearing. Alternatively, a deacon, server, or another concelebrant could momentarily bring forward a handheld mic so that the speaking concelebrant's hands remain free. Some concelebrants hold a microphone while speaking their assigned part, but this makes it impossible for them to extend both arms. Whether holding a mic or a leaflet, a priest oddly gesturing with one hand threatens to distract himself and others from prayer.

Other concelebrants remain silent and do not gesture at this time. They would appropriately stand with hands joined.

Deacons at the altar kneel for the epiclesis and consecration; they may assist with incense (CB 155). In the absence of a deacon, concelebrants would perform neither of these functions because of their priestly duties during the eucharistic prayer; however, one or more servers may assist with incense.

Concelebrants begin to speak and make gestures with the epiclesis. They pray this part of the eucharistic prayer aloud, but in a low voice. Two reasons stress the importance of this low volume: so that the presider's voice can be heard, especially if he is the bishop; and for the comprehension of the people (GIRM 218, CB 155). Depending on the size of the church and the number and placement of concelebrants, they may have difficulty reciting the words in unison with the presider. At times, even with only one or two concelebrants, their strong voices may overpower the presider's. The concelebrants speak in muted tones so that the presider may set the pace for the prayer. The people, too, are expected to participate in the eucharistic prayer by listening to its words and taking them to heart. They can do this best if they hear one voice leading them.

Speaking in a low voice is counterintuitive to many priests either because of their usual leadership role or their familiarity with the instruction from the Order of Mass to pronounce the words of consecration "clearly and distinctly" (e.g., OM 89). In concelebration, however, that instruction applies only to the presider. Reciting quietly in union with the presider also avoids the theological dilemma that Thomas Aquinas and others faced in the Middle Ages—if one priest recites the words of consecration before the rest, who consecrated? Because of simultaneous intention, the consecration happens simultaneously, but this is best evidenced when all recite in unison and the presider's voice predominates.

Seemingly contrary to this principle is the "praiseworthy practice" of singing the eucharistic prayer, including the parts assigned to concelebrants (GIRM 218). Yet even here, if the priests are singing in unison, the voice of the presider is to be heard above the rest. It is hard to imagine how this is accomplished except with a microphone for the presider and a disciplined group of priest singers.

At the epiclesis, as the concelebrants begin speaking together, they extend their hands "toward" the offerings (GIRM 222a, 227a, 230, 233a). This differs slightly from the presider, who extends his hands "over" the offerings. When a bishop presides, however, the word for the concelebrants changes to "over": the bishop "and the concelebrants hold their hands outstretched over the offerings in Mass at the epiclesis before the consecration" (CB 106). A footnote elaborates the point: "At the epiclesis preceding the consecration the hands are to be outstretched toward and above the offerings" (CB 106, fn. 79). However, multiple concelebrants cannot all physically hold their hands "above" the offerings. This gesture probably applies only to those concelebrants closest to the altar, as does the rubric for deacons to stand "behind" the concelebrants (CB 153).

Concelebrants use both their hands for this gesture, not one. The epicletic interpretation of this gesture is new in the history of the Mass.[2] Prior to the council, the priest placed his hands over the offerings during the *Hanc igitur* section of the Roman Canon, which is not an epiclesis. After the council, the gesture moved to the following section, the *Quam oblationem*, which includes a prayer that God will make the offering "spiritual." Eucharistic Prayer I comes no closer to an expressed epiclesis than that adjective. As the concelebrants' gesture resembles hand-laying on occasions such as anointing the sick, reconciliation, confirmation, the consecration of chrism, and

[2] Tymister, p. 290.

ordination, its meaning is now epicletic, as is the presider's. Immediately after these words, each concelebrant closes his hands (GIRM 222b, 227b, 230b, 233b).

As the presider begins the words of consecration together with the concelebrants, he alone takes the bread and then the chalice into his hands. This fulfills the limitation that the principal celebrant alone makes gestures during the eucharistic prayer except at the indications given (GIRM 217). Similarly, the principal celebrant alone bows slightly for the words of consecration; the rubrics do not indicate that concelebrants do the same.

As the presider takes the elements into his hands, the concelebrants are invited to make a different gesture, extending the right hand toward the bread and then toward the chalice. They make the gesture "if this seems appropriate" (GIRM 222c, 227c, 230c, 233c). In practice, concelebrants commonly do make this gesture, but it is not required as is the one for the epiclesis.

Some priests extend their right hand with the palm to the side, others with palm down. There persists a debate over which is proper. The rubrics themselves make little distinction between the gesture at the epiclesis and the one at the consecration. The first is made "with hands extended toward the offerings" (e.g., GIRM 222a). The second is made "with each extending his right hand toward the bread and toward the chalice, if this seems appropriate" (e.g., GIRM 222c). From these texts alone, it appears that the gestures for the epiclesis and the consecration are identical. In 1965, however, the Vatican published a clarification in the first issue of the Consilium's *Notitiae*, which stated that the second gesture was indicative, not epicletic; hence, it preferred palm to the side, not down.[3] The article itself is interpretive, not legislative.

A reference to the same article appears in a footnote in the *Ceremonial of Bishops*. The paragraph it supports says not much more than the GIRM: concelebrants "hold the right hand outstretched toward the bread and the cup." The footnote, citing *Notitiae*, says more, advising concelebrants that "at the consecration the palm of the right hand is held sideward" (CB 106, fn. 79). A footnote such as this, which cites a non-legislative source, does not much increase its authority,

[3] "Documentorum explanatio," *Notitiae* 1 (1965): 143.

especially when the main body of the Ceremonial and the actual rubrics upon which it is based make no clear distinction between the gestures at the epiclesis and the consecration. Still, the Vatican's only clarifications on the matter have called for the palm to be held to the side, even though there is absolutely no historical precedent for such a gesture in any part of the Roman liturgy. The Byzantine liturgy actually permitted concelebrants to extend their hands palms *up* during the institution narrative.[4] A socio-political problem certainly had some influence as well: The extension of a single right hand with palm down at the consecration resembled too strongly a gesture associated with fascism.[5]

Officially the question remains unresolved. One view holds that repeating the gesture palms down shows the unity between the epiclesis and the consecration. Another view holds that different gestures demonstrate different purposes of parts of the same prayer. A third option presents itself: No gesture need be made at the consecration. The concelebrants extend their right hand "if this seems appropriate" (e.g., GIRM 222c). If priests within a diocese agreed to one of these three options at the consecration—palm sideways, palm down, or hands folded—they would at least provide a vision of uniformity for the rest of the faithful at prayer.

After the words of consecration, the presider shows the host and then the chalice to the people, and concelebrants look toward the host and chalice each time (GIRM 222c). The rubrics at times give inadequate direction to the assembly regarding their postures and actions, and the consecration offers an example. The presider is supposed to show the elements to the people; logically, the people should look at what he shows them, but that rubric is missing. Consequently, many people lower their heads, manifestly not looking while the priest shows them the elements. The rubrics explicitly keep the concelebrants from doing the same. They look, and they thus give an example to the people.

After showing the host and chalice to the people, the presider genuflects each time, and the concelebrants make a profound bow (GIRM 222c, 227c, 230c, 233c). Logically, this is when the people may lower their heads in adoration if they wish.

[4] Tymister, *La concelebrazione eucarística*, pp. 295–96.

[5] Tymister, pp. 296 and 303.

The presider alone introduces the memorial acclamation, and the people respond (e.g., OM 91). This is a dialogue between the presider and the people. Concelebrants do not participate in it at all. They remain focused on their prayer to God the Father. When priests concelebrate alone with their bishop, without the presence of the laity, for example, during a retreat or days of formation, someone has to make the memorial acclamation. In those instances, it makes sense for the concelebrants to respond. Otherwise, the acclamation belongs only to the people.

As the eucharistic prayer resumes, all concelebrants offer the next part with the presider. As before, they speak in a low voice, and this time they gesture with hands extended (GIRM 222d, 227d, 230d, 233d). In the first eucharistic prayer, the commonly offered sections include one where the presider makes a profound bow and, then standing erect, signs himself with the cross. Because this is offered by all the concelebrants, they make these same gestures (GIRM 222e).

The same eucharistic prayer includes one exception to the rule that concelebrants gesture only when they speak. While the presider alone prays for "us . . . your servants . . . sinners," he strikes his breast. All the concelebrants do the same, even though they do not pronounce the words (GIRM 224).

After the anamnesis and oblation, when the eucharistic prayer turns to intercessions, the presider or a single concelebrant gives them voice. Other concelebrants remain silent, hands joined.

As the eucharistic prayer concludes, a deacon elevates the chalice. Although the rubric is not clear, the deacon should probably receive the chalice from the presider. In the absence of a deacon, a concelebrant may lift the chalice, though it would be less necessary for him to receive it from the presider. If there are more than two vessels on the altar, only two are raised. The vessels remain elevated until the people have finished singing "Amen" (CB 158).

The presider intones the doxology. The Order of Mass says he does this "alone or with concelebrants" (OM 98). The same options prevail when the bishop presides (CB 158). This is another dialogue. The presider is not to sing the concluding amen, so neither should concelebrants. Consequently, the prayer comes to a more satisfying conclusion if the concelebrants join the doxology. Otherwise, they would take part neither in the doxology nor in the amen. In rare situations where concelebration takes place without the presence of lay people, it makes more sense for concelebrants not to sing the doxology so that they may sing the amen.

Similar rules govern the other six eucharistic prayers (GIRM 235). The GIRM only goes into this detail for the four of them wrapped within the Order of Mass. Concelebrants find their particular instructions within the texts of the other prayers.

The Lord's Prayer

The presider alone introduces the Lord's Prayer. All recite the prayer together, and as the presider extends his hands, the concelebrants do the same (GIRM 237, CB 159). The rubrics are silent about the hands of the people. Presumably, they keep their hands joined, but some people extend them as they observe the presider and concelebrants, who are reciting together with them every word of the same prayer. Concelebrants keep their hands joined during prayers that they do not recite aloud, such as the collect, the prayer over the offerings and the prayer after communion. Presumably they extend their hands at the Lord's Prayer because, as in the eucharistic prayer, they gesture when they speak.

At the conclusion of the Lord's Prayer, concelebrants join their hands while the presider offers the embolism with hands extended. The acclamation that concludes this prayer belongs to the people and the concelebrants alike, though not to the presider (GIRM 238, CB 160). He remains silent as all the others declare, "For the kingdom. . . ."

Therefore, three acclamations in close succession call for different reactions from concelebrants: They do not voice the memorial acclamation, nor the amen at the conclusion of the eucharistic prayer; but they do voice the acclamation that concludes the embolism following the Lord's Prayer. The presider remains silent for all three.

The Sign of Peace

The deacon invites the sign of peace, but in his absence, one of the concelebrants does (GIRM 239). Although many believe that the GIRM only allows a concelebrant to perform functions of the deacon in his absence, the GIRM rather strongly *expects* a concelebrant to perform this one. The command to give the sign of peace first belongs not to the presider, but to another ordained minister. The presider may give the command only when no other priest concelebrates and no deacon assists.

The presider gives the sign of peace to concelebrants near him, and only then greets the deacon (GIRM 239, CB 161). In general, concelebrants exchange peace only with those nearby.

Breaking Bread

Concelebrants may assist in breaking bread during the Lamb of God. The principal celebrant begins, but other priests may assist (GIRM 240, NDC 37, RS 73). Deacons may help break bread at a typical Mass; however, when a bishop presides, they are not mentioned. Instead, the bishop begins, and concelebrants continue (CB 162). Presumably in a situation without concelebrants, a deacon may assist the bishop at this time.

The option for sharing this task appears even in the part of the GIRM that does not directly deal with concelebration (GIRM 83), which suggests that the breaking of the eucharistic bread may demand some time. The envisioned shared action supports the idea that all receive broken bread, rather than individual circular hosts, although these are not excluded (GIRM 321).

Receiving Communion

After the principal celebrant commingles the consecrated bread and wine, he alone says one of the quiet prayers in preparation for communion (GIRM 241). The Order of Mass indicates that he waits to say this prayer until the Lamb of God has concluded (OM 131). The concelebrants do not say this prayer of preparation.

All concelebrants must receive communion under both kinds (RS 98). Non-celebrating priests may always receive under both kinds (RS 99).

Receiving the host before "Lord, I am not worthy"

The concelebrants may receive the host in one of several different ways, either before or after "Lord, I am not worthy . . ." (GIRM 242). If before, they may approach the altar one by one, genuflect, and take the Body of Christ in their hands without consuming it. (This works best if there are few concelebrants, so that they do not carry the host some distance from the altar.) Or the concelebrants may stay in place as the presider offers them the paten from which they take the host without genuflecting. Or they may stay in place as one of the other concelebrants offers the paten in the same way. Or they may pass the paten from one to another and take a host, again without genuflecting and without yet consuming it. A deacon does not pass hosts to concelebrants.

When the bishop presides, there is another possibility. He may hold the paten as the concelebrants approach him one by one. In this case each of them genuflects before the bishop and receives the Body of Christ from him, without immediately consuming the host (CB 163). Usually a concelebrant makes a genuflection only if he is approaching the altar to take a host, not if he is receiving a host from another priest. When a bishop presides, the instruction to genuflect reminds one of the instruction that "the bishop is greeted with a deep bow by the ministers or others when they approach to assist him, when they leave after assisting him, or when they pass in front of him" (CB 76). Apparently to avoid a misplaced sign of respect, the priests approaching the bishop at this time make their sign of reverence to the Blessed Sacrament, not to the bishop.

In receiving the Body of Christ from the bishop, the priest does not take it from the paten as he does when he approaches the altar or receives the extended paten from another priest. The bishop gives it to him.

All the aforementioned options are in force only if the priests receive the Body of Christ before reciting the prayer, "Lord, I am not worthy." Thus, in all these cases he receives the host but does not immediately consume it. In no case does a person say, "The Body of Christ" to the concelebrant who receives the host (RS 98).

Once they have the host, the concelebrants are to hold it in their right hand, with the left hand underneath (GIRM 242). Although the GIRM does not make the connection to Cyril of Jerusalem, the norms for communion under both kinds in the United States does. "When receiving in the hand, the communicant should be guided by the words of [the fourth-century] St. Cyril of Jerusalem: 'When you approach, take care not to do so with your hand stretched out and your fingers open or apart, but rather place your left hand as a throne beneath your right, as befits one who is about to receive the King' " (NDC 41).

The concelebrants should all receive a host consecrated in the same Mass. When presenting the rubrics for Mass without concelebration, the GIRM notes that the priest is bound to do this (GIRM 85). It repeats the same point when he is about to receive communion (GIRM 157). At a concelebrated Mass, "the principal celebrant takes a host consecrated in the same Mass" (GIRM 243). This phrase is plainly copied from the non-concelebrated Mass. In truth, this paragraph does not explicitly state the same about the concelebrants. Even the preparations for a concelebrated Mass list a chalice of sufficient size or several chalices, without explicitly mentioning the number of hosts (GIRM 207b). The norms for distributing communion in the United States similarly call for the preparation of enough wine for the concelebrating priests, without mentioning the hosts (NDC 31). However, the CDWDS later made it clear: "The Communion of Priest concelebrants should proceed according to the norms prescribed in the liturgical books, always using hosts consecrated at the same Mass and always with Communion under both kinds being received by all of the concelebrants" (RS 98). The footnote cites the requirement that a priest receive a host consecrated at the same Mass. The very directive implies that other hosts may have been placed on the altar, although the GIRM never encourages the practice.

The presider alone raises a host slightly above the paten or chalice and begins "Behold the Lamb of God." Everyone, including all the concelebrants and the presider himself, says, "Lord, I am not worthy" (GIRM 243). As usual, the presider says quietly, "May the Body of Christ keep me safe for eternal life." Each concelebrant says the same quiet prayer (GIRM 244).

The presider receives the Body of Christ. He may not intinct his host into the Precious Blood. Even without concelebrants, the GIRM has the presider consume the Body of Christ before taking the chalice to receive the Blood of Christ (GIRM 158). Clearly this responds to the double imperative from Jesus himself, "Take and eat. Take and drink." In a concelebrated Mass the principal celebrant is to receive communion "in the usual way," as he does in a non-concelebrated Mass (GIRM 248).

The English translation of GIRM 248 is less clear than the Latin. It says, "the principal celebrant receives Communion under both kinds in the usual way (cf. no. 158), observing, however, the rite chosen in each particular instance for Communion from the chalice; and the other concelebrants should do the same." This could be read to mean that the presider may choose intinction as a rite in a particular instance, and the concelebrants have the same option. A more literal rendering of the Latin does not support this interpretation: "the principal celebrant receives Communion under both kinds in the usual way (cf. no. 158), having been preserved, however, the rite chosen for Communion from the chalice that the other concelebrants follow in individual cases." The other concelebrants may be following a rite different from that of the principal; that is, they may receive by intinction, tube, or spoon, as detailed in GIRM 245.

Thus, even if concelebrants receive communion by intinction, the principal receives "in the usual way," that is by drinking from the chalice, but leaving enough behind for the concelebrants to intinct (GIRM 249).

In these first scenarios, the concelebrants are already holding their own host, so they each consume the Body of Christ when the principal celebrant does.

The principal celebrant says the quiet prayer, "May the Blood of Christ keep me safe for eternal life," and drinks from the chalice. If there is a deacon, he receives both the Body and Blood of the Lord from the principal celebrant, even before the concelebrants receive the Blood of Christ (GIRM 244). The principal celebrant then leaves the chalice on the altar or hands it to a deacon or a concelebrant before the principal celebrant goes to a station to distribute communion to the faithful (GIRM 246a).

The concelebrants may drink from the chalice in one of several ways. They approach the altar individually or in pairs. Each genuflects, lifts the chalice from the altar, drinks, wipes the rim with a purificator, and returns to his place (GIRM 246a). Or they remain in their place as a deacon or concelebrant presents the chalice to them. Or they pass the chalice from one to another (GIRM 246b). The one presenting the chalice to the priest does not say, "The Blood of Christ" (RS 98). After consuming, either the concelebrant or the one presenting the chalice wipes the rim with a purificator.

At Mass with the bishop, a deacon presents the chalice to each concelebrant and wipes it with a purificator (CB 164), though a footnote permits the other options available when a priest presides. The concelebrant genuflects only if he has approached the altar, not if the chalice is presented to him by a deacon or priest.

No intinction is envisioned if the priest has received the host before the words, "Lord, I am not worthy." This avoids the precarious situation of a priest walking some distance with a host in his hand to reach the chalice on the altar. If intinction is to be an option, the procedure described below pertains.

Receiving the host after "Lord, I am not worthy"

Alternatively, the concelebrants may receive *both* the Body and the Blood of Christ from the altar *after* saying, "Lord, I am not worthy." In this instance, they have not received the Body of Christ before the dialogue begins, nor do they consume the host at the same time as the presider.

After the presider's communion, he gives the Body and Blood of Christ to the deacon. The elements are arranged on the altar, the chalice to the side on another corporal. The concelebrants approach, genuflect, consume the Body of Christ, move to the side without genuflecting a second time, and consume the Blood of Christ (GIRM 248).

They may drink directly from the chalice. Only concelebrating bishops and priests may pick up the chalice and drink from it themselves (NDC 44). Deacons and laity do not share the same liberty.

The GIRM also permits receiving the Blood of Christ by means of a tube or a spoon (GIRM 245). These methods are not much in use.

Alternatively, the concelebrants may receive communion by intinction. At the same Mass one may see some concelebrants intinct while others drink from the chalice. Intinction is one of several methods available to them (GIRM 245), but the Missal implies that intinction, if practiced at a given Mass, applies to all the concelebrants (GIRM 249). Indeed, where it speaks of the rite "chosen" for the concelebrants (GIRM 248), it does not presume that the concelebrants have chosen it individually. More likely, those who prepare the liturgy may choose intinction for all of them, due to reasons such as the provision of only a small quantity of wine for the Mass.

For intinction, the principal celebrant drinks from the chalice, leaving enough of its contents for the other priests. The deacon or a concelebrant sets the chalice next to the paten at the center or side of the altar, the vessels resting on a corporal. Concelebrants approach one by one, genuflect, take the Body of Christ in hand, and "intinct it partly into the chalice." Each holds a purificator under his mouth as he consumes in order to catch any drips. Then they each return to their places, though one concelebrant administers communion to the deacon in the same way, intincting the host for him (GIRM 249). (There is no provision for a layperson or even a deacon to self-communicate by intinction.) This detail shows that if communion is by intinction, all the clergy receive this way, the concelebrants and the deacon alike. Although in practice some concelebrants individually choose to intinct their host, they may be fraying the visual unity that even the method of receiving communion signifies.

Distributing Communion

For the distribution of communion to the faithful, the presider may enlist the assistance of concelebrants when the number of communicants so warrants (NDC 37). These concelebrants must each receive communion before distributing it to others (RS 97).

After Communion

As the communion of the faithful draws to a close, any remaining consecrated bread and wine needs attention. For the hosts, the usual options continue: The presider may consume leftover hosts at the altar, presumably with the assistance of concelebrants, or he may carry hosts to the tabernacle (GIRM 163, 279). At Mass with the bishop, a deacon or a concelebrant brings leftover hosts to the tabernacle and carries the paten or ciborium to the credence table to be purified over the chalice (CB 165).

A deacon may consume what remains of the Blood of Christ at the altar (GIRM 182). Concelebrants may assist (GIRM 247, 249). In practice, they often drink the last contents at the credence table or even at the communion stations. Coming to the altar, though, brings a sense of completion, reminding all communicants that even when receiving at a station, they receive, by extension, at the altar. The same ministers may help purify the vessels. The GIRM twice mentions that this is carried out at the credence table, not at the altar (247, 249). Elsewhere, the GIRM permits purification at the altar or in the sacristy after Mass (163), but it prefers the credence table (279).

Purifying vessels away from the main altar shows the lesser importance of this action compared with others carried out on the altar. Therefore, a priest would appropriately let a deacon or instituted acolyte purify the vessels to show that the action is not essentially presidential. Current legislation in the United States does not permit extraordinary ministers of holy communion to assist.

If fragments adhere to the fingers of a priest, he "should wipe his fingers over the paten or, if necessary, wash them" (GIRM 278). At Mass with the bishop, "if need be, [he] washes his hands" (CB 166). No similar provision is made for concelebrants. Although some sacristans have placed a vessel of water on the altar for a concelebrant to wet his fingers after receiving communion, the GIRM never recommends it and seems to deem it unnecessary.

The Concluding Rites

The principal celebrant leads the rest of the Mass. Concelebrants remain at their places (GIRM 250).

If Mass concludes with a solemn blessing or prayer over the people, the deacon commands them to bow down for the blessing. In the absence of a deacon, one of the concelebrants may speak this line.

The same is true of the dismissal. In the absence of a deacon, a concelebrant, rather than the presider, may dismiss the assembly.

The presider and the deacon kiss the altar (GIRM 251, CB 170), but the concelebrants do not. Instead, they make a low bow to the altar as at the beginning of Mass. The reason for this is not clear, except that the procession out of a church is less significant than the procession into it. For example, the GIRM indicates that the opening procession may be led by incense, accompanied by song, and include the *Book of the Gospels*. But none of these elements is mentioned for the procession at the end. In a similar way, the reverence that concelebrants give the altar is simplified, now that the celebration of the Eucharist has been completed and the community sent forth.

Neither the GIRM nor the *Ceremonial of Bishops* indicates clearly what reverence concelebrants give the tabernacle at the end of Mass. If the tabernacle is in the sanctuary, "ministers genuflect when they approach the altar and when they depart from it" at the beginning and end of Mass (GIRM 274). One could argue that this includes the concelebrants when the tabernacle is in the sanctuary. Or, as seems more likely, their reverence could be restricted to a bow to the altar because they do not genuflect to the Blessed Sacrament if they are moving in procession (GIRM 274).

All the ministers walk out in the same order in which they entered (CB 170). Concelebrants then follow the deacons and precede the presider.

The Sacristy

Upon reaching the sacristy, all ministers, including the concelebrants and the bishop if he presides, make a reverence to the cross (CB 170). Presumably, this means that they bow to the processional cross. "Then the concelebrants bow to the bishop and carefully put away their vestments" (CB 170). This fits with the practice that ministers bow to the bishop when they approach or leave him (CB 76). Consequently, the concelebrants make three separate bows at the end of Mass: toward the altar, the cross, and the bishop.

Sometimes the bishop may lead an acclamation at the end of Mass. While bowing to the cross, he may say something like, "Praised be Jesus Christ," to which all respond, "Now and forever." In some places, a dialogue ensues in Latin. As all bow to the cross, they say, "*Deo gratias.*" Then the bishop may say, "*Prosit,*" to which all respond, "*Pro omnibus et singulis.*" In English: "Thanks be to God," "May it be good," "for all and each one." This may hold some devotional appeal, but no such dialogue appears in the rubrics.

All are expected to observe silence in the sacristy after Mass, "out of respect for a spirit of recollection and the holiness of the house of God" (CB 170). Yet, as during the time before Mass begins, many concelebrants rejoice to visit with one another or friends from various parishes. This important time of visiting is best done apart from areas where others are trying to observe a prayerful silence.

When all has been completed, the GIRM gives an instruction to the people of God that surely applies to concelebrants as well. When Mass concludes, they "go back to doing good works, praising and blessing God" (GIRM 90c).

Other Concelebrations

Concelebrants have a special role at certain other liturgical celebrations. For example, at the ordination of priests, all the priests present lay hands on those being ordained. This applies not just to concelebrants, but to priests in choir dress as well.[6] They remain alongside the bishop, though without blocking the view of the faithful. At the end of the ordination rite, just before the Liturgy of the Eucharist, all the priests, or some of them, give the kiss of peace to the newly ordained.[7] Again, the rite does not distinguish concelebrants from non-concelebrants at this time.

At the chrism Mass, near the end of the prayer of consecration, all the concelebrants extend their right hand toward the chrism.[8] This does not apply to non-concelebrating priests in choir dress or unvested in pews. The chrism Mass is one of the most important occasions for concelebration with the bishop, and the introduction to the celebration presumes that the priests present are concelebrants.[9]

At confirmation, during the prayer for the coming of the Holy Spirit, concelebrating priests extend their hands toward the candidates only if these priests are actually to assist the bishop in administering the sacrament.[10] If the bishop alone confirms, then he alone extends his hands for the prayer.[11]

[6] "Ordination of Priests," *The Roman Pontifical* (Vatican City: Congregation for Divine Worship and the Discipline of the Sacraments Vox Clara Committee, 2012), 130.

[7] "Ordination of Priests," 136.

[8] *The Order of Blessing the Oil of Catechumens and of the Sick and of Consecrating the Chrism* (Washington, DC: United States Conference of Catholic Bishops, 2019), 25.

[9] *Order of Blessing the Oil*, 1.

[10] *The Order of Confirmation* (Washington, DC: United States Conference of Catholic Bishops, 2016), 24–25.

[11] During the Easter Vigil at St. Peter's in Vatican City, Pope Francis has invited all priests to extend their hands while he offers the confirmation prayer over the neophytes. However, there is no explicit permission for this. See my article "On Paper

On Good Friday, there is no concelebration. The service is not a Mass; hence, the only one who wears a chasuble is the presider. If other priests are present, they may wear choir dress or an alb. If they have a role in the proclamation of the Passion, it would be fitting for them to wear a stole. They do not prostrate with the presider. They take on the role of deacons only in the absence of deacons, but they remain vested as priests. At communion, they receive from the presider, who *does* say the words, "The Body of Christ," because they are not concelebrants.

---

and on Air: The Books and Broadcasts of Christian Initiation in the Age of Pope Francis," *Liturgy* 33:2, 11–19, DOI: 10.1080/0458063X.2018.1412209; https://paulturner.org/wp-content/uploads/2018/03/Christian-Initiation-in-the-Age-of-Pope-Francis.pdf.

Conclusion

Celebrating Mass is a priest's most visible and sacred duty. Indeed, for all Catholics, participating at Sunday Mass is their great responsibility, privilege, and joy. The Eucharist is the source and summit of life. Priests especially send their roots deep into the Eucharist so that their branches may bear good fruit.

The Eucharist is the center of a priest's activities, the place where he gathers the members of his flock. He shares time and ministry with many of them during the week, so the eucharistic gathering brings all together to praise God, to celebrate faith, and to seek divine help for service in the week ahead.

Priests become focal points of unity at the Eucharist. They effectively collect the prayers of the people and present them to God because they have come to know their needs. Often before Mass a congregant will approach the priest with a request for prayer. It may be for a sick member of the family, a friend who has died, a search for a job, or some personal trial. Becoming aware of the human stories behind the human faces at church helps a priest put more intentionality to the words his says.

As the presider for both the Liturgy of the Word and the Liturgy of the Eucharist, the priest lets both these elements guide his interactions with the faithful. He applies the word of God to pastoral situations demanding spiritual insight. He builds up the communion of the church through his work with societies, committees, and families.

Michael Begolly showed the interdependency of pastoral ministry and parish worship:

> The presider can more effectively lead the worship of the community when there is an ongoing relationship between the presider and the assembly. This sense of trust is developed in the

> day-to-day interaction of the presider with the community, and is deepened through the presider's pastoral care of the community. By coming to know the community in its daily life, the presider leads the community in bringing to worship its joys and sorrows, its struggles and triumphs.[1]

Two other sacraments require the administration of a priest: reconciliation and anointing of the sick. In a similar way, they show the priest who he should be as a person even outside the liturgy. Priests are ministers who reconcile, helping those with opposing views to find common ground. They are ministers of healing who bring new insight and health to those who are broken and spent. Because they daily live out these vocations of forgiving and healing in open interactions with the people of God, they celebrate with them more intimately the sacraments of forgiveness and healing as well.

The ministry of priesthood is the lifeblood of one's *ars celebrandi*. Ministry puts a priest in conversation with God and the people. It assigns him responsibilities within communities. It draws out his abilities to listen and to judge, to create and to heed. His interactions with people will lend authenticity to the style of his presiding. His presiding will form him as a minister who brings word and communion to the people.

The Eucharist is the source and summit of life because it gathers a priest's ministry into a ritual that follows the mind of the church even as it incorporates the personal gifts that God bestows uniquely upon each priest.

As the revised English translation for the Mass was making its debut in 2011, ICEL, which provided most of the work on the project, released an interactive catechetical DVD on the Eucharist, *Become One Body, One Spirit in Christ*. Therein, the Very Rev. Canon Alan Griffiths contributed an article on *ars celebrandi* that concluded with these words:

> Art, beauty, celebration: in the Catholic Church, God communicates to his people something of the divine life. It is a communication in sacrament. Within the community which he calls into

[1] Begolly, *Leading the Assembly in Prayer*, pp. 38–39.

> being, through graced human acts and words, by the work of the Holy Spirit, Christ imparts to his people a participation in the dynamic engagement of creative love that is the Holy Trinity. He does this that the world may believe.
>
> Human acts and words are crucial to this mystery, just as human flesh was to the divine Word. And to speak of human acts and words is to speak of their authenticity, their quality, their deliberateness and reverence, in short, their art. The *Ars Celebrandi* is nothing less than our participation in the gracious circle of the work of God.[2]

Whether the priest is presider or concelebrant, he holds this great mystery in his hands. He pursued his vocation as an invitation from God; he celebrates Mass as an invitation from the church: to preside over the sacred mysteries both with faithfulness and art.

[2] Alan Griffiths, "Presidential Prayers and Practice: Towards an *Ars Celebrandi*," *Become One Body, One Spirit in Christ* (Ottawa: International Commission on English in the Liturgy, 2010), DVD.